6/72

Saint
Martin de Porres

MANY SIDED MARTIN
... THE FIRST NEGRO SAINT OF THE WESTERN HEMISPHERE

by
Marieli and Rita Benziger

Cover design by
J. Daniel Woodward

BENZIGER SISTERS, *Publishers*
466 E. Mariposa Street
Altadena, Calif. 91001

Printed at Nagle Printing Co. Inc., at Flagstaff, Arizona, United States of America

Here we have a saint who definitely belongs to our western hemisphere. In many ways he reminds us so much of Francis of Assisi, his great love of human beings, of nature and animals.

Marieli Benziger

Contents

INTRODUCTION

In 1935 having read the French book on the life of Martin de Porres I decided here was our Saint, a negro, and at that time I wrote a half a dozen different articles for the Inter - racial Review. The title of my article was "American Pioneer" who had built the first new world college. His purpose was to educate the down and out. This champion of the afflicted started an Agrarian reform—a back to the land movement with the planting of fruit trees and olive groves. Another time I wrote an article in 1938 headed "Father of Four Hundred Thousand Orphans." The mothers in those days rid themselves of their babies by tossing the little girls into the Rimac River of Lima, Peru. Martin de Porres established the first foundling homes of the new world. That was way back in the early seventeenth century.

Strange as it may seem, this great holy man was only canonized on May 6, 1962 by Pope John XXIII.

I asked myself why this delay of recognizing the sanctity of such an outstanding personage and every person I talked to in Europe told me it was racial prejudice. Already on September 16, 1668 Pope Clement IX had tried to have his cause for canonization introduced but all efforts failed.

Century after century was to slip past. 1763—Pope Clement XIII; in 1836 Pope Gregory XVI; and on June 9, 1926 Pope Piux XI, all these great men had tried to introduce the cause for canonization of a Peruvian negro. Pope Pius XII told us in February 1946 that it was his greatest wish to see this negro canonized.

I brought my articles and my book on Martin de Porres to Cardinal Patrick Hayes of New York City and asked him where I could find out more about Martin de Porres. He remarked to me, "I too have wanted to see this negro canonized. Go to Rome and speak to a certain Cardinal who has lived for a long time in Peru. Question him as to the reasons why so many centuries have slipped by without Martin de Porres being elevated on the altars of the Church." It was this Cardinal in Rome who told me point blank that this had been a deliberate sabotage from within.

He gave me several instances where the necessary material had been assembled and was to be deposited in Rome, but orders from within had been given to "throw overboard any and all material that can be of use in Rome. We don't want a black man canonized from Peru."

Here we have a saint who definitely belongs to our western hemisphere. In many ways he reminds us so much of Francis of Assisi, his great love of human beings, of nature and animals.

Marieli Benziger

1
Gold

What more fascinating background for a story than the Andes? The Andes — an impenetrable fortress of gigantic rocks erected by nature to guard the Golden Treasures of the Sun God. Ancient Peru stood hemmed in on the east by the stupendous cordillera of the Andes, flanked to the west by the gray-green waters of the Pacific Ocean. Hundreds of years before Columbus was born, Peru—then known as the Inca Empire—was the seat of a fabulously wealthy civilization. To the newcomers, members of the white race, its history would remain forever one of mystery.

The Supreme Ruler of this Indian tribe of llama-herders and potato-growers was known as "The Inca." By members of his limitless Empire, he was looked upon as a Direct Descendant of the Sun God. He called himself the "Son of the Sun." His rule was characterized by benevolence. His entourage outdid in splendor anything conceived of. Egypt with its Pharaohs paled before the riches of this Mountain Empire.

Throughout the centuries, the Inca rulers had the welfare of their subjects at heart. They were social-minded. Each citizen worked according to his particular station and was appropriately rewarded for his efforts. The Inca kings were geniuses at organization. Buried away from outside assistance, with their own limitless resources they erected an Empire unequalled in history. Nothing was overlooked, nothing omitted.

What they had they wrested from the soil. They were tillers, toilers. Yet they felt perfectly safe. From the ocean they knew no invaders would broach their mountain capital. For Cuzco was safely situated 11,000 feet above sea level. Everywhere they erected fortresses. Machu Picchu —two days away by fleet-footed

1

messengers—was a sky fortress, a town perched on the sides of a mountain with its storerooms, temples and palaces scattered on terraces and connected by 3,000 stairways. To centralize and stabilize their resources, the Empire was interlaced with 2,500 miles of stone highways. There were innumerable footpaths across which nimble messengers sped and inter-communicated. Suspension bridges swung across mighty chasms, linking mountain to mountain.

Along the coast, skilled masons erected gaily-painted adobe cities. In the highlands there were imposing towns of superb masonry. Cuzco, the capital of the fabulously wealthy Inca Empire, was a city of unparalleled beauty. The walls of the temple erected to the Sun God were pure gold; gold were its huge doors, roofs and gardens. The gigantic fortress of Sacsahuaman was built of immense stones cut without the use of steel implements and fitted together without mortar or cement. So close were these rocks placed that not even a blade of grass could be inserted between them. The Great Inca had his throne out in the open— a vast parade ground before which he reviewed his warriors and his workers. Near the throne of The Inca were the grandstand seats for his Royal Retinue. This was cut from stone.

His magnificent palace, as well as the homes of his subjects, were decorated with gold and silver. The precious metals were also used for the table as well as in the kitchen for cooking utensils. Even the llamas had their harnesses decorated with golden trinkets. Next to the palaces were great baths and The Royal Inca had his own. The winter months were long and cold. Out of the rock a sort of toboggan slide had been hewn. Whether for utility or pleasure was never to be known.

With great pains, able engineers terraced the mountains. The Inca rulers realized that not by gold alone could their subjects survive. Every inch of land was parcelled out to farmers. The mountainous soil was carefully cultivated. The terraced hillsides created by man were watered by means of irrigation channels. Here were grown sugarcane, cotton and vegetables of all kinds—especially the indispensable potato and fruits. Each town and village, besides its temples, palaces and homes, had vast storehouses. Here the guardians of the law stored ample supplies, forestalling drought, famine or war. Neither poverty nor want was ever known to these thrifty, frugal and farsighted people.

Within that mighty Empire, 10,000,000 peace-loving Inca Indians lived. They were clad in finely-woven garments ornamented with beautiful jewels of gold and silver—often embellished with featherwork. Gifted in the fabrication of priceless textiles, they wove equally well with cotton or wool. They embroidered designs of beautiful hues—a technique which intrigues the 20th century lover of art. They mastered crocheting and knitting, using with ability the wool of the llama or the vicūna. The highlanders were able craftsmen in pottery and stonecarving as well as the hammering of gold and silver.

While the Inca Indians were pursuing their contented existence, living off a soil from which their ancestors had wrested subsistence for centuries, Spanish adventurers were seeking gold. They had crisscrossed the uncharted seas—goaded by that insatiable thirst for treasure. Their galleons blazed trails on the Atlantic and Pacific. Unsuccessfully, they had explored the unconquered regions of the North American continent. In the name of the Spanish Crown, they had acquired land. But that land was sterile of the gold they sought. Like men in a dream, they were goaded by the lure of gold — ever before them. Ships were lost, men died in the New World without accomplishing their aim. They fought amongst themselves like jealous fiends because gold was not forthcoming.

Spanish *conquistadores* were risking life and limb in the Northern continent of the New World. In the Southern continent, gold was so plentiful that the Inca never considered their treasure extraordinary. There nestled the plateaus—rich with priceless metals— closely-guarded by nature's watchtowers. Jagged peaks blanketed by everlasting snows formed a perpetual shroud that kept all enemies at bay. Thus the independent Inca Indians lived with utmost security, enjoying the seclusion of their fertile valleys.

3

These powerful tillers of the soil were a stalwart lot. Their well-regulated lives bespoke prosperity. There was beauty in the landscape. The beflowered mountain slopes had flourished for centuries before. No grasping foreigner, no dangerous enemy had ever so much as caught sight of this kingdom within its rockbound fortress. There was nothing to fear as haughty llamas replenished royal coffers with gold and silver. Was not the Mighty Inca worthy of riches and honor? He, the Son of the Sun God, was carried in a litter ornamented with precious gold and lined with plumes of tropical birds of varied hues and gorgeous butterflies. His robes were regal—resplendent in flaming scarlet. Members of his suite were attired in contrasting colors, emerald and gold. The plumes of thousands of parrots, parrakeets and macaws, as well as those of tiny hummingbirds, were used by them to make themselves attractive to the Imperial Eye.

Thus the unwanted guest or curious stranger had never scaled the rocky buttresses, nor leaped across giant canyons. There was only one secret pass leading to the great plain thousands of feet in the sky. Cuzco was absolutely safe. It had been for centuries. Besides gold, the Empire was rich with the life-giving potato. Both the white and the sweet potato grew abundantly. Yearly vast quantities were stored by the army as a tribute to The Great Inca against famine. The Indians had their own method of preserving the potato crop. First cured by frost, when thoroughly frozen the potatoes were dried in the high altitude and bright sunshine of the Andes. Thus they could be stored indefinitely.

The heralds who doomed this happy land were shipwrecked sailors. Their discovery of gold was to bring desolation to an entire Empire. These men were to ring the knell of Peruvian Glory. A Spanish vessel foundered off the dangerous Peruvian reefs. Indians witnessing the disaster plunged into the surf, dragging the half-drowned crew to safety. If the Incas had stood by and let these Spanish perish, they would have averted the disaster that was soon to descend upon them.

Astonished at finding the natives bedecked with golden necklaces and armbands, the Spaniards learned much about the metal they were seeking. They murdered their benefactors, buried their remains and hastily departed on foot to bring the good tidings. The surviving sailors traveled northward across the scorching Isthmus, across the Spanish Main. When they reached Mexico, the news spread like a forest fire. There was gold! Gold had been found in South America! To prove that they had not merely seen, but had handled the long-desired gold, they carried samples with them of Inca workmanship.

Means of communication were slow. Somehow the word got to Spain. Ships at once set sail for the Inca Empire. The greed for gold was to lead these Spanish adventurers to commit one of the most abominable crimes in history. Francisco Pizarro headed the Spanish Expedition. Cold-blooded, appallingly cruel, this representative of the King of Spain finally sighted land. With merely a small band of picked followers, he landed—occupying Peru in the name of his sovereign, Charles V.

Suspicious that an ambush might be laid, he personally reconnoitered every inch of ground. Aided by the former shipwrecked sailors, he sought in vain for the mysterious mountain trail. At last news was signalled to the two hundred waiting warriors. Pizarro had found the trail that was to lead to ultimate victory. Aboard the galleons there were forty horses. These were made to swim ashore.

Heading his soldiers, Francisco Pizarro led the *conquistadores* across territory never before penetrated by the white race. Slowly, cautiously, the cavalcade followed its master. What had seemed a zigzag footpath got lost in a narrow passage between the mountains. There remained nothing but the dried bed of a former torrent. The path through the gorge was about to be abandoned. One of the more intrepid soldiers refused to turn back. Persevering, he rushed back breathless. The treacherous pass had widened into a magnificent road.

Amazed, the *conquistadores* fell on their knees. Never in their homeland had they seen such a magnificent stone highway. Great boulders had been flattened. Gigantic blocks of rock lay side by side, making an excellent boulevard. Up this mountainous highway climbed the weary cavalcade of two hundred men. One by one, the lamed horses limped painfully along. Fearing permanent injury, Pizarro commanded a halt. The horses— unaccustomed to hard pavements —had not been shod for miles and miles of rocky roads. Their shoes became worn. A blacksmith was ordered to shoe the horses. The Spaniard had come unprepared for this emergency. Discovering silver in a nearby mine, he shod the restless animals with silver horseshoes!

Pizarro had been unmercifully criticized by his fellow countrymen for loading his galleons with horses. It was unheard of folly. Was it not sufficient risk to stake the lives of men? Pizarro had carted fodder and built special quarters for his cavalry. Pizarro's farsightedness was to provide the climax of the Expeditionary Force. It was not to be the prowess of *conquistadores*, nor the clanging of their coats of mail, nor their banners flying in the breeze that brought a Spanish victory. The clatter, clatter, clatter of the horses' hoofs upon the pavement was to strike horror and terror. Hannibal with his elephants, crossing the Alps, had accomplished the same results as did Pizarro with his cavalry. Superstitious Indians with their slow, plodding llamas fled in terror.

In panic they fled to their fortified cities, recounting tales of a vast army. They had heard the echo and reecho of strange noises. Monstrous beasts with shining armor were bearing down upon them. They, the peace-loving inhabitants of the soil, were outnumbered. Terrorized by these rumors of an apalling army, The Mighty Inca and his warriors decided to capitulate. But not before they retired to the Temple of the Sun God—there to spend the day in prayer and fasting.

The Sun God showed his displeasure by hiding his visage behind great snow clouds. On the 15th day of November in the year of 1533, a blizzard pelted the invaders, halting their march. Pizarro goaded his men to advance. He realized that if they did not reach shelter before night, the campaign would be stalled till spring.

Cross in hand, under the pretext of introducing Christianity, the treacherous Pizarro sought for an interview with The Mighty Inca.

Pleading that his mission was one of peace and good will, the Spaniard and his *conquistadores* gained admission to the Andes Empire. The Great Inca, wishing to avoid bloodshed, consented to capitulate. What was Pizarro's price?

Pizarro pointed to a vast room. That room—a chamber twenty feet square—was to be filled with gold from the floor to the ceiling. Two smaller rooms were to be filled with silver. Then he would be contented. The 10,000,000 Inca Indians and their powerful ruler might continue in peace if they embraced Christianity. Perhaps the latter clause was Pizarro's method for stilling his guilty conscience. The Spaniards had been amazed at the beauty of the town before them. Cuzco was a fairy-tale city.

An army of Indians went into action. They carted golden vases, utensils and trinkets to the chamber to be filled with gold. They did the same with the silver. The *conquistadores*—astonished at the fabulous wealth, at the facility with which the spoils had been collected—held a secret consultation. They had no scruples. The Mighty Inca must be disposed of. In cold blood, they murdered King Atahualpa.

Then began a period of plunder and spoliation. Crazed by the sight of such wealth, they became cruel beasts—murdering, raping, looting, destroying. Within six weeks, a mere two hundred Spaniards captured the most entrancing of all empires. The Inca Mountain Empire was liquidated. To them nothing was holy or sacred. Homes, temples, palaces were stripped and burned. Men, women and children were done away with. No nation had ever paid a weightier ransom. An independent, fearless people were enslaved overnight.

Crazed by their successes, the Spaniards had but one ambition—gold, yet more gold. Higher and higher piled the loot: priceless tapestries, artistic textiles, golden and silver articles of every shape, size and kind.

Not satisfied with robbing, the conquerors set the natives to manning the mines. Night and day, day and night, the Incas dug mountains of gold and silver. There were not enough galleons to transport the treasure. Llamas were too few and slow. Human beasts of burden could be forced to form an unending caravan. Upon the backs of Inca Indians the weighty burden was placed. Barefooted, they trudged northward—Mexico their goal—the proud, once-happy and contented peoples now broken. The architects, masons, craftsmen and engineers who had been the pride and glory of their Empire found themselves doomed to life sentences. The trail they left behind them was a trail of tears and blood.

Hundreds of thousands, nay millions, formed the cortege that transported the gold that was to fill the coffers of the monarchs of Spain. Heat, cold, disease, hunger, thirst depleted this enslaved people. The Isthmus which connected the two American continents became whitened with blanched bones—the bones of 40,000 exhausted Incas who perished along the Spanish Main while carting gold to Mexico. In less than ten decades, the Incas—who had numbered 12,000,000 souls—were obliterated. The Spaniards had for all time blotted out the greatest, the most flourishing civilization of the Western Hemisphere.

To satiate their thirst for adventure and fortune, thousands of Spaniards flocked to this newly-founded colony. This motley mixture consisted of priests and pirates, of soldiers, knights-errant and cutthroats. There were the young; there were the old. Lima became to them the center of the Universe—a Universe of Gold. Francisco Pizarro was the hero. He was sent back to take full charge.

In 1535, two years after his conquest, the ever-increasing number of Spaniards prompted Pizarro to erect a capital. He chose Lima on the banks of the Rimac River, encircled with the foothills of the Andes, to become the City of the Kings. Twenty-five miles inland, away from the sandy desert, a great city sprang into being overnight. On the ashes and ruins of an Ancient Civilization, the white race was to start its own.

2
Out of the Past

Ana Velazquez was rightfully proud of her beautiful adobe home. Few women in Peru could boast of anything lovelier. It was a mixture of Spanish and Inca art. Her world of happiness was filled to overflowing. She had everything a woman could wish for. From morning till night she sang, voicing the tunes her mother had taught her as a child. She had little work and few responsibilities. Don Juan insisted that the household duties be confined to slaves. Was he not rich? Did he not have gold? Why should her soft, velvety hands become rough and coarse?

Reticent and shy, Ana preferred the solitude of her thoughts to the noisy prattle of neighbors. With satisfaction she sauntered through the cool patio. In the garden the fronds of palm trees rattled with the evening wind. Arrayed in one of her loveliest dresses, she hid herself under an arbor of rainbow-hued morning glories. The flowers had begun to fold their petals for the night. She counted the ever-ripening bananas. Unknowingly she crushed the brittle nasturtiums that had outgrown their bed.

She studied the hedge of fiery geraniums. They had become taller than her man. This massive hedge formed a useful barrier. Here she shut herself away from a world she looked down on. There was gossip in town. There was jealousy. To her it mattered not. She had a kingdom of her own within which she ruled as queen.

Her charm, her grace, her lithe spirit had run away with the heart of Don Juan de Porrez. Since their arrival in town, he had become its most respected citizen. The Spanish Crown had learned of the disorders in Lima—a town barely forty-six years old—founded by Francisco Pizarro after the destruction of the mighty Inca Indians. Strife, murder, lawlessness had to be curbed.

9

His Gracious Majesty had named one of Spain's outstanding noblemen, a Knight of the Order of Alcantara, to head the military garrison. Naturally Ana was jealous of her lover. She wanted him to herself. She did all in her power to hold him, to make his home everything he could desire.

Living as she did on Espiritu Santo, one of the busiest thoroughfares of the city, Ana often sought the shelter of her garden. There midst her flowers and her birds she dreamt dreams. All day the hummingbirds darted in and out. Gaudy butterflies fluttered aimlessly amongst pansies and violets. Screeching parrots impertinently mocked her.

Often as Ana lay on her reed couch, she relived the past. How she longed for her mother, wishing she were alive. The future had been different from anything anticipated. Her mother had been distrustful. She had constantly warned her only child to be careful of the white race; to have nothing to do with the Spanish conquerors.

Though Ana and her mother had been slaves, she had never known her father. She was faintly suspicious that the man her mother never mentioned had been a Spaniard. A streak of good fortune won both their freedom. Slaves on a Panamanian plantation, their master had decreed on his deathbed that they were to be freed. Ana had been born in Panama. The New World was the only world she knew. Her mother's story had been very different.

Only a few years after the colonization of South America had Negro slavery been introduced. The work in the mines and the using of natives to cart cargo across the South American continent had caused the rapid decimation, the final extinction of the Indians. There were no longer sufficient day laborers, miners, artisans or masons to build homes; farmers to dig fields. Negroes were then imported from Africa. They were strong. They had great powers of endurance.

After Columbus had discovered the New World, King Charles V was the first to permit this human traffic in 1517. Monopolies of licenses were granted by Spanish monarchs for the importation of Negro slaves.

10

It is said that in one single year, over 97,000 were torn from home and country to be transported to Spain's new colonies. Surprised by great white birds that suddenly appeared on the horizon, the natives flocked to their beaches. Instead of knowing fear, a childlike curiosity filled them at the wondrous sight of the beautiful birds floating majestically on the waters.

When white men landed on their shores, they had been cajoled with signs and gifts to come aboard. Those that had resisted were rounded up like wild animals—bound hand and foot and thrust into corrals. Lashed into submission, they were stripped of all they had. Their heads were shaved; their nails cut to the quick. More dead than alive, quivering with terror, they were thrown into the dark hatches of vile and stenchful galleys.

Ana's mother was never to forget the horrors of that journey; that African homeland she would never see again. Until her death, the bloodcurdling yells of dying victims startled her nightly sleep.

Week after week the galleon cruised the ocean. The captain had miscalculated. Their meager rations of food and water ran low. To save the healthiest and huskiest, Negro prisoners were brought from the hold; then forced to jump into the sea. Some, crazed by lack of water and the appalling heat, did so gladly. Others had to be seized bodily and thrown overboard. Their cries of anguish, as fathers and mothers, brothers and sisters were cruelly separated, were something Ana's mother never forgot, never forgave.

By the time their galleon reached Panama, two hundred companions had found a watery grave. Only a tiny group remained to be sold to the highest bidder. Thus had Ana's mother become the property of a plantation owner.

Ana had always been spellbound by the sea. She spent her leisure hours midst the wharves, gazing at the giant galleons. The Spanish armada reminded her of brilliantly-plumaged birds, floating gracefully in Panama Harbor. She liked to watch the changing of the guard, their shining coats of mail, their flying banners. Sometimes she followed them through the city to the Church of San Jose with its golden altar. Panama was indeed the proudest city of the New World. There was constant traffic, constant coming and going.

On one such occasion, she had noticed a handsome Spanish officer. She recalled having seen him before; perhaps at her master's table. He had always entertained the nobility and officers. His plantation was noted for its open hospitality.

Ana had picked him out from a motley crowd of treasure hunters. Their lack of breeding, their cruel coarseness made them hated and despised. To her the nobleman seemed very different. His brawny strength, the sharp clear-cut features, his stately walk had captivated her attention from the first. One Sunday, coming out from Mass, they met. He had noticed the quiet, unusually attractive maiden. Halting at a flower booth, he had bought her an armful of roses. Her gay smile, her dazzling white teeth, her flashing eyes conquered him at once. He had never seen a lovelier creature.

Don Juan de Porrez had renounced riches to obey a royal command. He had left in Spain both family and friends, as well as the ancestral castle. In Panama he was lonely. Wearied by the coarse jests of ribald soldiers and sailors, with relief he sought the companionship of this mere child. He claimed her matchless beauty, her charm bewitched him.

As their acquaintance ripened into friendship, its permanency seized Ana with panic. Her conscience reproached her. Her mother's dying words were branded in her mind. What if her mother's premonition had been true? What if this smouldering passion burning within her breast was merely one-sided? Afraid to face her thoughts, Ana sought peace from the struggle within her by escaping. She fled to the country—all the while hoping against hope that Don Juan might find her.

For three days, Don Juan de Porrez sought the girl he loved. He missed her quiet presence. At last her hiding place was found. His amber-brown eyes were clouded with displeasure.

"Why have you done this to me, my little flower? I thought I had lost you. . . that perhaps you had gone forever."

Filled with apprehension and doubting her own strength, Ana refused to answer. She tried to avoid the candid stare of the Spaniard.

"Would it not have been better had you lost me? Better for you and better for me?"

Don Juan, who had always had his own way in life, fumbled nervously: "You must never do this to me again. This has been most upsetting. Just as I thought I had you — like a butterfly you flit out of my life."

Ana looked up shyly. "Why would you be upset? Surely there are others. . . your own kind."

"Florecita mia, let's not argue. I feared you had deserted me." His tapering hand, denoting his cultured background, drew Ana towards him.

Ana was still afraid. "Are you sincere? Can I trust you?"

Laughingly he pulled her close. "How dare you doubt the word of a nobleman? I place my life, my honor, all I have at your feet. What more can you want?"

Ana gazed at the marble whiteness of his hands. She could not resist. Her love was far too great. She laughed, her melodious voice sounding like the music of bells. "Do you always have your way?"

"This time I intend to, whether you like it or not. What do you say to this?" He drew her closer, clasping her in his brawny arms.

Trembling like an aspen leaf, Ana clung to him. Then the fear that had enveloped her vanished. Tossing her proud head and sighing deeply, she revealed: "I'm no longer afraid. I'll never run away. I'll never leave you."

Don Juan was satisfied. The velvety softness of her warm flesh thrilled him. There was healing in her soothing caresses. As he held her hands, he said: "They remind me of tulip petals, darling. You must always be my flower."

To Ana there seemed nothing strange in the fact that she, who was the color of the night, and he as waxen as parchment should love each other. Don Juan showed her deference. There was no one he liked being with better than with Ana.

The months that ensued passed like a dream. Hers was the triumph of loyal devotion. Even her whims and her caprices were carried out. Ana, in turn, studied her lover. She knew him like an open book. She delighted in the realization that nothing would ever come between them to mar their happiness. Don Juan reaffirmed his affection. Ana's smile worked wonders.

The fleet anchored at Panama. As Don Juan boarded his galleon for inspection, he was handed a dispatch. Late that afternoon he galloped through the sweltering tropics. Ana had his favorite cooling drink waiting for him. "Why this hurry?" she asked.

Don Juan was disturbed. "Bad news," he growled. "His Sovereign Majesty has named me to head the military garrison in Lima. There is discipline to be maintained. I've been appointed to that outlandish post." He tossed aside his riding whip. He paced the floor. A man of varied moods and fiery passion, he cursed and raged.

Ana had never seen him possessed by this sort of a demon. "Surely you do not have to go. You're free to refuse, to reject the offer."

"That's how much you womenfolk know about military discipline," he scoffed. "I'm leaving at dawn tomorrow. I must be off to pack my belongings."

Suddenly the full force of the impending action of her lover dawned on Ana. Horror-stricken, she realized he was about to abandon her. She knew that if she let him slip out of her life, she'd be like all the other women along the wharves who waited, mourning the loss of lovers who would never return.

Seizing Don Juan's arm, she cried: "What's taken possession of you? Have you lost your mind? Do you think I'm staying behind?"

"Of course you are," he snarled. "A galleon's no place for a woman."

Ana pleaded. She argued with a mother's patience. . . analyzed his former professions of love. . . switched the conversation to his career. "Surely you are free to renounce your military career. Why not become one of the landed gentry? Buy a farm, run a sugar plantation?"

"Darling, it's useless arguing with you. What can you know about life, its possibilities?" Brusquely he pushed aside the tear-stained girl. Anger made him cruel.

14

Ana stifled a cry. He had hurt her.

"Were your words empty, hollow promises? You swore you'd never abandon me. Now you are about to stalk off as if you'd never known me. The test has finally come. We were to share our joys and sorrows. Now you're willing to discard me like some worn article of clothing. . . to fling me aside like a faded flower. . ."

Don Juan disliked scenes. He could not bear tears. They made him ashamed of himself. He failed to calm the brokenhearted girl.

"There is nothing I can do. Can't you see I'm just as distressed as you are?"

Ana flung herself on her knees. Realizing her lover was about to go, she implored: "Take me along. You can't live alone. You'll need a housekeeper. If you found Panama—the greatest city of the New World—lonely, what will you think of Lima? Don't be heartless, cruel. I could never live without you. If you had only listened to me. Or if I had only insisted. . ..we would have had a church wedding. The old padre consented to officiate at our marriage. But you. . .you. . . never carried out your promises. . ."

Don Juan had always prided himself on being a man of honor, for keeping his word. He fully realized he'd been in the wrong. Ana's tears prevailed. Reluctantly he acquiesced. Ana could accompany him. Ashamed of his cowardice, he sought to make amends.

Ana, loving, forgiving, quickly pardoned—but only time would heal the wounds she had endured that day. She wondered if, perhaps, her mother had not after all been right.

Aboard the galleon room was made for Ana. A certain sense of triumph filled her with contentedness. Though the voyage had been stormy, she had enjoyed every moment of her first long trip. How different her experience had been from the sorrows endured by her mother—conquered, enslaved by this same race of white men. But there was too much to see, too much to learn for her to be engrossed in somber thoughts and meditation.

Each day brought its added pleasures. The thousands of sea lions barking and browsing on rocky coasts. The hundreds of thousands of birds of all dimensions and colors. Playful porpoises chasing each other as they dipped in and out of the Pacific. When the wind was slack, there was fishing. One hundred miles offshore, giant turtles were found floating, paddling in the water. No matter how sultry or hot, no sailor dared plunge into the shark-infested waters.

Before she knew it, the harbor of Lima was reached. Herds of llamas transported both cargo and travelers across the two-hour sandy stretch. Lima, with its churches, palaces and numerous homes, was a strange medley of Spanish and Inca architecture. Don Juan had picked out a suitable residence for himself and for Ana. He wanted a home that was worthy of his exalted station and rank. Close to the lovely church of Espiritu Santo Don Juan bought a house. To prove the sincerity of his intention, he gave it to Ana. They would live there. They would make Lima their home forever.

Ana felt secure. Her reverie under the morning glory arbor was interrupted by the clatter of hoofs. Instantly she was on her feet. Her drowsiness had vanished.

With great strides, Don Juan swept through the patio. "Ana, darling. How I've missed you." He kissed her warmly.

"How I wish I were a man," she sighed. "I would never be parted from you for a moment. Dearest, look at your boots. You're covered from head to feet with dust. Are you not tired?"

"No, my little flower. Not tired—just glad to be back home again." He proudly looked around the garden. "Nothing in Cuzco remains as beautiful as this. Only ruins, ashes, devastation. Our warriors did their work of destruction mighty thoroughly. I'll be hanged if I can see what was their purpose. Selfish greed leads nowhere."

Ana caressed away the wrinkles on his forehead. "Come, now. Forget about the expedition to the Inca capital. Tell me, now that you are home, what you plan to do."

One of the slaves bowed low. "Master, you left this on the saddle."

"Why, of course. . . of course. I forgot I had an important bundle—a surprise for you."

Ana gave a cry of delight. "For me? How like you—to remember I was in the valley while you were scaling the Andes."

16

"Darling, how could I ever forget you? You're ever-present in my mind—both waking and sleeping."

Quickly Ana loosened the palm-leaf wrapping. She clapped her hands with joy; then flung across her shoulders a crimson-fringed shawl outlined with exquisite needlework. "Just what I have been wanting ever since I was a child! How could you have guessed?"

"Whenever I see someone wearing a beautiful shawl or jewel, I always think how much better it would look, gracing the shoulders of my *florecita*. So. . . you like it?" He beamed his approval.

Together, shunning company, they ventured into the nearby mountain passes. Not only did Ana keep Don Juan amused; she tenderly ministered to him when he was sick. Malaria and tropical diseases held no terror for her. From Inca vendors she bought the bark of the quinine tree. She administered the bitter-tasting dose to her protesting patient. Ana was firm. To her Don Juan was but a child to be treated with firmness and vigilance. His speedy cures roused the curiosity of the garrison. The soldiers envied the well-groomed official who kept to himself.

Sometimes Ana condescended to carry a woven rush basket of self-produced dainties to one of the neighbors. Yet outside visits were rare. She and Don Juan were far too engrossed in their own personal lives to seek happiness elsewhere.

Life in Lima—called the "City of the Kings"—had been colorful, even eventful. It was all that it had promised to be. Then one day, a peremptory summons ordered the commander of the garrison to report with his troops in Mexico. Political factions in that far-off colony were at war. The Spanish Crown insisted that peace be established. Don Juan de Porrez was assigned the difficult mission.

This time Ana realized that though Don Juan's absence might be long, it was only temporary. Grieved at leaving his loved one and home, he promised to be back soon.

Then came the final day for departure. The streets resounded with the tramp of marching feet. The bells of the twin-towered Cathedral pealed the tocsin. Loud and long it called the war cry. Across the palm-lined Plaza de Armas, Don Juan led his troops.

They were reviewed by the Viceroy in person.

On to the coast they marched. There fully-armed men-of-war tugged at their anchors. Ana, with other women from the garrison, watched spellbound while the embarkment of the flotilla of heavy square-rigged sailing ships took place. These floating castles resembled turreted fortresses. Great guns were mounted on the upper decks. Flags fluttered at the handsomely-carved stern. Sailors scrambled to release anchor. Some climbed the mizzen; while others tugged the rigging or grappled the tacking.

Ana gazed tearfully into the distance while they disappeared on the nothern horizon. Then she wrapped her crimson-fringed shawl around her proud shoulders and she and her maidservant returned home.

3
A Visitor

After Don Juan's galleons sailed northward, Ana waited. Patiently she counted the days. Her self-made calendar announced that soon he must be turning homeward. No word of his arrival, no word of his whereabouts reached her. She spent long hours in the dimly lighted church next to her home. She lit candles, begging the Madonna to pity her, to hear her. Yet her lover stayed away. Anxiety turned to grief. Fear clutched her heart. Had Don Juan perished? Would he never return?

The days, the weeks, the months dragged by. It was as if she were chained to the gallows and neither saw the sun nor felt its warmth. Her garden was overgrown with weeds. The birds were more plentiful. They were never disturbed. She never heard their song, nor smelt the perfume of fragrant roses. Bananas rotted on the tree. Torrential rains poured through the leaking roof.

Ana heard nothing, saw nothing, felt nothing but the gnawing pain of waitfulness. Her ears were deafened to all sound but the wistful expectancy of a familiar footstep, which never came.

Ana faced hard times. The funds for household needs were depleted. She had dismissed her servants. Others who had the means could at least feed them. She had barely enough to eat. Though discouraged, she was confident that Don Juan would return. Her wrongs would be righted; her needs cared for.

She busied herself with household duties. Reticent, shy, she preferred to live in solitude. No prying eyes were to detect her poverty and want. She waited till the women of her neighborhood had drawn their water. Then furtively she darted through the forsaken alley. She filled her huge earthen jug with icy water. With grace, with ease she poised the awkward burden on her shoulder.

Head erect—she returned home, bruising the geraniums as she hurried through the hedge. Passersby often stopped to ask who was this stunning woman. Yet Ana never paid attention to any on the street. She was too engrossed in thought.

As she looked back over these eight months of torture, she wondered if anyone had suffered as she had. Her loneliness was now somewhat alleviated by the realization that soon she would share her empty home with a tiny visitor.

Together she and Don Juan had often discussed the joy of having a son. He wanted an heir. Someday their child would inherit the grim castle he had abandoned in Castile. Together they would introduce him to the gay court life. As son and heir of a Castilian nobleman, he would share in his father's titles and honors. Did not Don Juan—a Knight of Alcantara—trace his lineage to the fighters of Alcantara? To the men who wrested Granada from the Moors? Though temporarily there might be poverty and even want, life would right itself with Don Juan's return.

Lovingly Ana prepared the swaddling bands. Too poor to buy a layette, she got out her loveliest shawls. Nothing would be too good for Don Juan's firstborn.

At the appointed hour, Ana was suddenly seized with fear. She was afraid to be left alone. Hailing a street urchin, she sent a messenger to fetch Ana de Escarcena. Her hour had come. Throughout the hours of the night, the two women watched and waited. At dawn, the stillness of the early morning was broken. The lusty cries were those of a newborn infant. Ana had become a mother. In her arms she held a boy, Great was her joy. Don Juan had wanted a son.

As was customary, Ana's child was carried in state to the Church of San Sebastian the very day of its birth. The kindly parish priest, Padre Antonio Polanco, waited at the baptisimal fount in alb and stole, holding a lighted candle.

The ritual full of mystic meaning was intoned; the words of exorcism pronounced over the sleeping infant. Thrice the Sign of the Cross was traced. Its lips tasted salt—symbol of wisdom; the oil of catechumens upon its frail breast a sign of Eternal Life. The head was annointed with Holy Chrism, denoting participation of the Christ-Life. Finally, the triple-pouring of water—baptising Martin in the name of The Father, The Son and The Holy Ghost.

After the ceremony, the padre invited the godparents to the rectory. There on the 53rd Page of the Parish Baptismal Registry, he entered the following: "In the Year of Our Lord 1579, on ninth day of December, baptised Martin whose father is not known. Child of Ana Velázquez, now a freed slave. Juan de Huesca and Ana de Escarcena—godparents." Antonio Polanco signed the notation.

From then on, Ana's life revolved around her baby. Its needs were few. Yet its arrival had revolutionized her life. Once again she had something to fill the aching loneliness. Her lovely voice sang the melancholy tunes she had learned from her own mother. As Baby Martin's cradle rocked in the patio, Ana weeded. Her soft hands became calloused and cracked.

Everything had a new meaning. The pain that gnawed gradually became less bitter. Time healed the wounds. Though the months stalked on, Ana stilled the fear that she and her infant might never again meet the Spaniard who had filled her life with such exquisite happiness.

On the last day of September, the church bells of Lima rang out their joyful clarion. At that late hour of the afternoon, the sandglass showed the Angelus was not yet due. Every bell in town pealed loud, pealed long. Word spread. The fleet had arrived in port! Ana prayed, prayed as never before. "God. . . bring me back my Don Juan."

Then followed the tune of martial music, the tramp of marching feet, the clatter of cavalry. Ana rushed to the street. She was afraid to look. Could she bear the thought that he might not be amongst the returning garrison?

As the military parade came nearer, everyone craned his neck. As she raised her eyes, she met those of a plume-bedecked official so tanned by the tropical sun that he was hardly recognizable. Before she knew what had happened, Don Juan had swept her off her feet; had clutched her to himself and embraced her affectionately.

"Ana! Ana!" he exclaimed. "The waiting has been cruel, been long. I could hardly contain my impatience."

"I feared that you would never return," she whispered tremblingly.

He looked at her closely. *"Florecita mia,* have you grieved for me?"

She nodded, bursting into tears. The unexpectedness of the joy was too great.

"Ana, don't. . ." he murmured tenderly. Holding her hands, he looked at them with amazement. "What's happened? My darling. . you've aged." '

There was much to tell him. Of grasping creditors who had hounded her doorstep. Of merchants who had taken advantage of her good faith and honesty. Of the resulting penury.

Don Juan was furious. He would teach these men to mind their own business. He would right the wrongs she had endured.

"I must go to report to the Viceroy. These papers have to be in his hands before night falls. But I'll be back as soon as possible. We'll go out tonight. We'll celebrate by feasting and dancing. Everyone shall see that you're my lady; that I am proud of you." With that he turned his horse, gallantly waved his feathered hat; then galloped down the road.

Ana roused herself. Could she have dreamt that the unbelievable had actually happened? Was this a mirage? Coming to her senses, she realized that the suddenness of Don Juan's arrival had pushed her baby to the background. She had forgotten to tell him of the birth of their first-born.

One of the neighbors was asked to send an older child to keep watch over Baby Martin. Ana was going out. She did not wish to leave him alone. She put on her fullest skirt, while underneath stretched layers of stiffly starched petticoats. Over her head went her *mantilla*—held high by a wooden comb—the last bit of finery she had clung to.

Ana dressed her toddling son. Then waited. It grew late; too late for the child to sit up any longer. She proudly laid him to rest. To her he was the handsomest child in town.

It was late, very late when Don Juan finally reached the house. He had been detained by the Viceroy. The business had been urgent. Trouble was brewing. At any moment, there might be a riot right in the heart of Lima. He'd been distributing his orders.

Within the house, all was dark save for an oil lamp. Its wick sputtered. A few stray embers on the hearth glowed.

Placing her fingers to his lips, Ana led him to a wooden crib. "I have a surprise for you. For nine interminable months, I've waited to show you our treasure."

Don Juan would not be silent. "Ana. . . tell me, is it a son? Have you given me what I so desire. . . an heir?"

The sleeping child awakened. It was good natured. It cooed. It called to its mother.

When Don Juan learned that he had a son, emotion hushed him. It was what he had most longed for, wanted more than anything else in life—someone to bear his name, someone to whom to hand the de Porrez escutcheon when his fighting days were over.

Ana lifted her precious child. Martin toddled nicely. In a second, both father and son were together. Baby Martin's warm little body cuddled lovingly in the arms of the kneeling man.

"Darling. . . if I had known what was waiting for me, wild horses could not have held me back. Night and day you've been with me, but I never suspected you'd have this gift awaiting my arrival."

The adobe room was dark. The flicker of the oil lamp was so faint that it cast the merest reflection on the adobe wall. Outside crickets shrilly cried. Otherwise there was silence.

Don Juan played with his baby. Ana watched the two with beating heart. The moment she had so hoped for had come. The two who meant more than life itself were one. The father and the son. She noted that the soldier had caught the frail little hand in his great brawny one. She was struck by the contrast—the whiteness of the one, the darkness of the other.

"Ana!" cried Don Juan. "Bring me that light."

His voice was so hoarse, so strange, that she was afraid. She could not imagine what had happened. Mechanically she did as she was told. She turned up the wick. She placed it on a table.

As if possessed by some strange sinister power, Don Juan roughly seized the child. He had never handled a baby before. Little Martin cried loud and lustily. He had been frightened and hurt.

"Why. . . what's the matter?" asked Ana. "You must not handle a baby like that."

Don Juan had caught Martin, staring at his features. With a sneer he flung the baby at her. "You liar! You cheat! Pretending that nigger is my son."

Ana stifled a cry of horror. She had so trusted his love that never for a moment had the racial difference ever caused her any anxiety.

"What do you mean?" she asked, approaching him, still clinging to her badly-frightened child.

He snarled: "I'll have you publicly whipped and turned out of town. That black bastard is no son of mine. I am a member of the Spanish nobility. Don't pretend that this is a scion of the Royal House of Castile! That little black scoundrel is the child of some black devil, not mine. You'll never prove that to me or any legal authority."

Ana had lost all power of persuasion. Don Juan raved like a maniac. The house shook. His diabolical pride had been hurt. He knew there was no de Porrez blood that could be that color.

"As far as I am concerned, you can starve. If you ever come near me again, I'll have the roof burned over your head. No punishment could be harsh enough for your infidelity. Never again will I cross the threshold of this cursed home. Nor do I wish to set eyes on either you or that ugly crow."

Don Juan seized the lamp, using it to find his way to the door. Then, stumbling in a panic of rage, he flung it on the adobe floor where it crashed and burst into flame.

Rodriguez, the neighbor's son whom Ana had asked to mind the baby while she went out, had heard the scene from the patio. As the room caught fire, he rushed into the street calling for help. Ana, with her usual presence of mind, groped for the earthenware water jug and extinguished the flames. Then, sobbing, she collapsed on the ground.

For days, the stunned Ana walked about in a daze. Paralyzed with grief, she neglected Martin—the cause of her sorrow.

Sometimes she tried to reason within herself as she relived the stinging remarks. Don Juan had loved her; had professed his admiration, his affection. She was dark—the same color as her infant, who strongly resembled her. The child was hers. And, what was more, it was his. The laughing, amber-brown eyes belonged to Don Juan. Now that the anguish of waiting had come to an end; now that Don Juan was back, he'd have nothing to do with either the woman or child.

Ana's faith in her Castilian lover had been rudely shaken. It was as if a dagger stabbed her each time she thought of him. The wound he had inflicted was deep. She had once worshipped the ground he walked on. She had been insistent that he was incapable of evil. Yet he, who had been the hero of her waking and her sleeping hours, had now become the villain who had wrecked her life.

Sometimes, for hours on end, Ana would stare at Baby Martin. She wondered how anything so sweet and innocent could be the cause of such sorrow.

Some of Don Juan's friends came to visit Ana. The rumor spread. Everyone felt pity for the brave mother. They reassured her that his outburst of anger had been only temporary. He was such a fiery, hotheaded Spaniard, time would cool and alleviate his hurt pride.

Ana was in doubt. Surely no sane person could act as her lover had. Pride. . . that inordinate, selfish pride. Had it not wrecked the lives of other girls she'd known? She was not the first whom a white lover had abandoned. They were a strange lot, these Spaniards. They thought nothing of courting, of making love with girls of her dark color or that of the Indians. They were ardent, passionate lovers with suave promises on their lips. Yet they refused to accept the consequences of their acts or to bear the responsibility for rearing their own dusky offspring.

As the weeks lengthened into months, Ana despised the very life she led. Don Juan was still stationed with his garrison. He lived in town not far away. Ana never saw him.

At times such hatred filled her heart that she was afraid of herself. Furtively she would look around, making sure no one was present to guess the evil thoughts that surged within her breast. Every vestige of happiness had been swept overboard. In one short hour, hopes and prayers of years had scattered and been shattered. There remained nothing but an empty void which she filled with bitterness; a sardonic hatred that fanned itself by petty meanness, revengeful cruelty. Hatred and despair had pried into her inner life. The loveliness of character that had once been hers was marred. A sinister shadow followed her. Ana was no longer herself.

What the future held in store, God alone knew. Her immediate needs were provided for. The charity of friends saw to it that there was food and fuel. The home Don Juan had given her sheltered her from the sun and rain.

The ever-reoccurring fear of hunger, the uncertainty of the moment, made her look about for means of earning a livelihood. She who had so haughtily disdained the poor wondered what she should do now. Women day laborers earned a few *centavos* treading and mixing underfoot clay and hay. But, working for masons who used this concoction in the manufacture of adobe homes was far from satisfactory. There was always cotton to pick, sugarcane to cut. Yet Ana knew she could not physically withstand the rigors of that sort of manual labor. Hers had been a sheltered and secluded life.

Her moods fluctuated. Hatred against Don Juan switched to his child. Why should she endure the anguish of loneliness? If Don Juan returned, she would be reinstated. There were ways of disposing of unwanted children. He was young, far too young to remember. There was the swiftly-flowing Rimac. That river was the burying ground for hundreds of unwanted Negro and Indian babies. The Rimac would guard her secret.

Whenever Ana had steeled herself to commit the act, she lacked the courage to accomplish the deed. Torn between the helplessness of the baby and the happiness that might again be hers, she sent little Martin away to board with poor people in the foothills.

4
All Alone

Painful years had passed. The appalling night of Don Juan's rejection had left a scar which marred Ana's life. No longer able to face the torture of conflict—that indecision of choice between her man or child—she succumbed. She sent messengers to Don Juan.

The Spaniard was back once more in the cheerful adobe home he had loved so much. But Ana never felt the same towards him again. No matter how ardently he protested he loved her, she doubted his loyalty. He had done something to her. In wounding her, he had killed the glow of life. She lived shrouded in a cloud of mistrust. Poor, simple, unassuming, childlike Ana had changed. Her faith in humanity was blighted for all time.

The second courtship lasted longer. Ana was no longer extravagant. She frugally salted away the gold that Don Juan lavishly spent on her and the household. He had deserted her once. He might do so a second time.

Her premonition that her security was not to be lasting was correct. After the birth of their second child, Don Juan left her—never to return. Juana had been named after her father. The baby girl was as dark as her absent brother. Neither of the children was ever to know their father. Thus, for the second time, the liaison was broken this time permanently.

The reestablished peace and prosperity soon disappeared. The incentive to live vanished when Don Juan left the house. Motherhood had been but secondary. Ana had only tolerated her offspring. Her jealous affection had been lavished too generously on the man she loved. There was no room left in her heart for maternal love. Her little ones were to suffer; suffer far more cruelly than Ana ever could.

The pretty adobe home became a revolting hovel. Dense vines cluttered the apertures which once had been windows. The door was closed in summer and winter, alike, to keep out a swarm of flies attracted by the rotting filth. The stench was such that only the most hardened could endure the odor. Ana, herself, was unrecognizable. Deception and suffering, ingnobly borne, had furrowed her face. She was called a witch or hag. Frightening was her presence when she shuffled her haggard and bent body.

To only a few do sorrow and even failure come as a challenge—the weak, cowardly and indecisive breaking under the strain, becoming embittered. Ana was true to type. It was as if her daily diet were wormwood and gall. She nursed discontent, jaundiced her mind as well as body. She succumbed to the disease of hating. The more she dwelt on past injustices, the more warped became her outlook on life.

She wasted neither time nor affection on Martin. When the lean, undernourished child returned home, she rebuffed him. She loudly upbraided and cursed him constantly. The daily floggings were a reminder that he, above all, was the curse that had wrecked a home. When there was not sufficient food to go around, it was Martin who did without. After all, it was he who was to blame for their hunger, their want.

No matter how hard Martin tried, he never succeeded in pleasing his mother. Any attempt on his part to be helpful, to sweep away the refuse that littered their path, caused her to fly into a rage. Undaunted, Martin persevered in his attempts to pacify her. Invariably he failed miserably, coming away with bruises for his good intentions. A burning brand would sear his body. The bamboo rod was broken on his back. If he ducked earthenware vessels, he escaped being struck by them. Agile and quick—he'd hide, returning home only when his mother's unleashed emotions had been somewhat pacified.

Home to Martin was a veritable hell. He lived in constant dread of punishment. The entire neighborhood gossiped and talked. They marveled at his gentleness of character, at his evenness of disposition. Martin became an object of admiration. He was a general favorite. Whenever he walked down the street, everyone had a kind word for him. They liked to see his radiant smile. For, no one could quite smile like Martin. He was like a sunbeam, radiating joy. His huge friendly eyes, his irresistible manner, endeared him to both rich and poor.

The quiet, serious child was different from the playmates of the gutter. Even when on an errand, he was followed by a group of children clamoring for him to join them. The noisy and the naughty gamins stopped their thieving if Martin joined them and told them stories.

Martin was poor, desperately poor. He was clothed in rags. He knew and tasted poverty. Perhaps that's why the poor were his favorites. Whenever he had anything to share, he would always divide with them. Even in his childhood, to Martin no racial barriers existed. Every home became his home. All peoples were his friends.

The Indian mother who had to cart the vegetables to market liked Martin. She entrusted her child to him—secure in the knowledge the infant would be well cared for. The old woman suffering from rheumatism—unable to drag herself from her couch—depended on him. At dawn he would sneak down the street to start her fire; to watch the boiling cauldron. He proved himself an excellent nurse, bringing her water with which to wash and sweeping her home. If there were a fight in the neighborhood, it was Martin who settled the dispute.

Thus, at an early age, Martin shifted for himself. By helping others, he earned his meals—often merely a crust of stale bread and sweetened cocoa. But to him it tasted like a royal feast. His mother's cruel curses had hurt; hurt more than he dared admit. But at last he was no longer a burden to her. This mere child miraculously managed to get enough food on which to live. From bitterness had come peace.

Things in the de Porrez home had grown from bad to worse. Neighbors, loud in their criticism of Ana's conduct, tried to rectify the evil. They remembered what she had once been; what she had become with time and want.

Doña Francisca Velez Miguel was approached by some of the townsfolk. She was asked to use her influence with Martin's mother. She had known Ana when she first came to live in Lima. She went to call and to investigate. What she saw convinced her that Ana needed help; that poverty and want were the root of much of the evil.

Doña Francisca had a small house. It was untenanted. She invited Ana and her children to come to live on the street called Malambo. The house was in good condition. If Ana accepted the offer by the end of the week, they could move. At first, Ana hesitated. But when pressed, she gratefully accepted the hospitality offered her.

Ana was no longer as loud or as violent in her accusations. Perhaps she was afraid her benefactress might learn of her conduct. Faultfinding had become a habit. She had little use for her son. She classified him as a thief and deceitful liar—a good-for-nothing from whom she could expect nothing. To a certain extent Martin was to blame. Yet it was not deceit, but generosity, that had brought about this accusation.

No longer caring to be seen in public, Ana would send Martin to do the shopping. When he returned from the market with fresh vegetables or a sack of potatoes, she was positive they had been tampered with. She would harshly demand: "How many have you stolen?" Martin would hang his head. "I have stolen none."

"Then. . . where's my change? What's the matter with you, anyhow? You seem to eat my money."

Martin would look at her with the reproachful eyes of his father. "Mother, there is no change."

"What! No change? You liar. . .you thief. Tell me what you've done with my money."

Each time Martin would hesitate; then stammer his confession. "There was a poor boy whose sister is dying of fever. There were five *centavos*. I gave them to him to buy medicine from an Indian at the market."

Ana shook him and then whipped him soundly. "That's what you get for disposing of my money. One day you give away a bunch of carrots; another time the onions. Now it's the money. When are you going to stop? This thieving will bring no blessing."

There was no resentment in Martin's heart. Somehow, in some unaccountable manner, he had hurt her feelings. It troubled him. Great tears welled in his eyes and splashed to the ground. "I'm sorry. . ."

"Sorry? Liar! You've told me that a hundred times. What's that filthy thing lying on your bed? I'd throw the cur out if he had not tried to bite me each time I approached him. Now get him out of here. And don't let me catch you bringing anything else into my house."

Martin was somewhat relieved. He'd find a home for the sick dog. As he went toward his cot, the dog wagged its tail and licked Martin's hand; then started growling and snarling. "Now stop. Stop, good dog," said Martin caressingly.

"Where is your blanket—the brand-new one that Dōna Francisca gave me?"

Martin had suspected as much. So she'd found out about that, too. "But mother. . .I thought she gave it to me. It was to be mine, she said."

"Yours? Nonsense! Nothing is yours. Everything is mine. I condescend to permit you to use it. Don't be impertinent. Don't you dare answer me back."

"It's with. . . the Indian woman," he stammered. "The poor sick old woman at the end of the street."

Ana laughed. Her cruel laughter cut deep in its cold heartlessness. "The Indian has been dead these three days. You brought a new blanket to a dead woman? Now I've caught you!"

"She was so cold, so poor, that I brought it to her the day before she died. She loved it. When they came to bury her, there was nothing in the house with which to wrap the body. . ."

Martin had no chance to finish the sentence before her mother interrupted. "So you let them bury her in my best blanket!" Then Ana had boxed both his ears. She shook him so violently that his teeth rattled—when, with a sudden shriek, she let go of the boy. A snarling sheep dog had flung himself upon her skirt.

Quick as a flash, Martin's two arms went around the dog. Gently he coaxed the animal to the door. As they reached the safety of the open air, Martin drew a deep breath. Again he'd escaped. He would find a new home for the stray dog.

The sensitive boy was torn between his desire to be helpful to his mother and his love for the poor. Though Ana constantly whipped him for his disobedience, it was quite unintentional. He just could not pass a beggar on the road and leave him empty-handed. He'd never been able to say "no" to any human need, to any impassioned cry for help. "No" was a word that did not exist in his vocabulary.

Thus Martin was always bound to be in hot water. To see him, no one would have believed he was only eight. Responsibility and suffering had aged the child, had matured him far beyond his brief years.

5
The Unexpected

Don Juan de Porrez had firmly made up his mind. He'd never again have anything to do with the woman who had presented him with two black offspring. Yes, he had loved her. He had enjoyed being with her. But, true to type, he ceased being concerned about her welfare.

To a Castilian nobleman, to a Knight of the great Alcantara, the very thought of having a Negro for a son was abhorrent. He'd even heard it remarked that the boy had begun to look like him. Of course it was a disgrace—an unfortunate disgrace which he never mentioned in letters home. The less his relatives in Spain knew about his actions, the better. Probably someday, when he wearied of adventure, he'd pick out a handsome woman of his own rank and station. She could bear him children and raise an impeccable family.

Don Juan had lived an eventful career. From Lima he had been sent to Santiago. This had enabled him to break all ties with Ana. His friends no longer had any excuse to work on his feelings. After a prolonged absence, he was called back to attend to business in Lima. While in town, his friends were determined to remind him of his neglected paternal duties. They told him all about the fascinating little boy; reproached him for his lack of charity. Obdurate, he refused to be bothered by any hard luck tales.

The men had recourse to Dõna Francisca Velez Miguel. Would she give a party? Her charity was proverbial. Perhaps at the end of the banquet, she might plan a sort of rendezvous. They left the details to her. This was not the first time she had come to the rescue of Ana and her brood.

Don Juan de Porrez accepted the invitation. The dinner was

attended by the outstanding citizens of Lima. The countless courses had been served in style. The numerous wines flowed generously. Everyone was in an exalted, jovial mood. No attention was paid to a diminutive lackey who helped remove the massive gold and silver platters. There were many servants and Martin had been eager to earn a few extra pieces of silver.

When the meal was finished, the guests rose to sit in the flower-scented patio. Doña Francisca asked Don Juan what he thought of the little lad who passed around the sweets and tobacco. Without the faintest suspicion as to the true identity of the undernourished child, the warrior held out his hand and helped himself to a cigar.

"This little boy is the son of Ana Velázquez." There was a wicked twinkle in Doña Francisca's eye. "I believe, Don Juan, you must have heard of her. She was renowned for her remarkable beauty in the days when you first came to Lima."

Don Juan stared. He was taken aback.

Doña Francisca carried on the one-sided conversation. "Martin, tell the gentleman something about your childhood. Do you remember where you once lived?"

Martin's eyes glistened. "Do you mean before you found a home for us? The house on the street of Espiritu Santo, where my mother and father lived."

"Do you remember your father?" asked Don Juan huskily, taking a sudden liking to the frank-faced lad.

Martin shook his head. He sighed: "No. . . I don't. But I wish I had."

"What difference would it have made had you seen him?" asked Don Juan.

"Then I'd know him when I met him. I'd go looking for him. I'd try to find him. Perhaps he's dead. My mother never speaks of him."

"What do you do? Do you go to school?"

"Oh, my no. We're much too poor. I run errands. I make money that way. This helps my mother, who never knows where our next *centavo* is coming from. Sometimes when there is a party, I help here—just as I am doing tonight."

"How's that? Why have you not started your schooling?"

Martin laughed. "You have to have money to be educated. The poor are not taught, Sir, to read or write." Why, if it had not been for Dōna Francisca, his mother and sister and he would have starved long ago.

"If you had money, what would you like to do?" Don Juan asked.

"I'd like to be a doctor. . . to take care of the sick. . . to sit up with the dying."

"Don't forget to mention," laughed Dōna Francisca, "that you'd give away your last *centavo*—even your wool blanket."

Martin could feel how he was blushing. The blood rushed to the roots of his hair. He wished she had not said that in front of the officer.

"Mother says I'm too stupid to go to school, that I'm too ignorant to learn. School, she says, is only for smart people. I wish I could read and write," Martin sighed. "Then mother might not threaten to send me away. No one on our street, Sir, either writes or reads."

The child's pitiful sigh did something to Don Juan. For the first time in years, he was moved. "If you want to be a scholar, there's nothing to prevent your becoming one. Someday you'll find the right person who'll pay your expenses."

All the while, the child was studying the face of the gentleman. Martin shook his head. "You're wrong, Sir. I was not joking when I said we were too poor. When you're hungry most of the time and know your mother and sister are, too, you don't think about an education. You just hope for enough food without having to worry where the next meal is coming from."

Martin had captivated Don Juan. The soldier suddenly felt remorse that he had never investigated the needs of his children. Without divulging his identity, he took a leather wallet from his belt. He opened it and handed Martin a large gold coin. "Take this, lad. You're an alert, bright boy. Get yourself some new clothes and buy your sister a present."

Martin's eagle eyes had noticed the beautiful wallet. "May I look at it?" he pleaded.

Don Juan gave it to the boy, who stroked it gently, feeling the softness, turning it over to admire the colors.

"Do you like it? Would you like to keep it as a souvenir of tonight?"

"Oh. . . may I?" gasped Martin.

"Yes, boy. And keep what's inside as well. There's a silver Rosary that I've carried these nine long years. You'll probably put it to better use than I ever have. One of these days, I'll send for you. We'll see about having you learn reading and writing."

Martin was so excited that he did not wait to thank the gentleman. He tore out of the house and down the street to his home.

To everyone in life comes the necessity for sharing a great joy. Without realizing what he was doing, Martin had banged the door behind him. It was late. . . far past bedtime. Ana knew he had been helping at the great house. She was annoyed by his lack of consideration, by the sudden noise. He'd awakened her from a sound sleep. She rose, administering a few well-placed blows. After all, there was nothing like keeping a boy in his place. Martin certainly needed it.

Ana's anger no longer had the power of hurting him. Martin's heart was singing. He was going to learn how to read! He would be able to write! Like the refrain of a well-known song—this thought flashed through his mind.

"Mother, don't be angry. . ." he blurted. "There was a nice gentleman, a grand gentleman at the party who said he'd help me learn how to read and write. He said he'd send me off to school!"

Ana was convinced the boy had gone out of his mind. She'd often wondered at his weakness of will. On second reflection, she decided it was merely another of his fabricated lies.

"What? You little black devil. . . read and write? Just who do you think you are to have such swollen ideas? Why, you're nothing but a brat. . . a dog of a mulatto. Who told you you had brains? Who fed you this nonsense? He was fooling, making fun of you. And you —you half-wit—believed him! Don't worry. . . your schooling is about to start, all right. The day after tomorrow, I'm sending you to the cane fields. Your bleeding hands will soon dispel these grand ideas. You'll grovel. . .grovel till the end of your days.''

Martin gasped—his mouth half-open with horror. Perhaps his mother was right. Perhaps the man had merely made fun of him. Then he looked down and realized he was holding the nobleman's wallet. That, at least, was real.

"What's that?" said Ana. "Give it to me!" she demanded. Her long, bony arm darted forward. Her sharp, cruel fingers clamped like a vise. The child's hand yielded to the pain.

Seizing the wallet, she hissed: "Who have you robbed? You'll have us all in jail yet—you good-for-nothing thief.''

"It wasn't stolen. . . it wasn't stolen," Martin sobbed hysterically. He had reached the breaking point. He could not stand the abuse, the tyranny any longer. "It's mine!" he pleaded. "Give it back to me.''

With a loud clatter—the large gold piece fell to the floor and rolled under the table. Ana bounded after it. Years had passed since she had seen so much money.

"What's this? Who'd be fool enough to give a beggar like you a gold piece worth a workingman's yearly wages?''

"The gentleman I told you about. It's for me to keep. . . for me to use.'' Poor heartbroken Martin knew his hopes for secreting some of the money had gone. The friends who were even more destitute than he would never see a single *centavo* of it now that his mother had seized the gold.

Ana turned the wallet in her hand. She noticed something familiar. "Who gave you this?" she shouted shrilly.

"I don't know. A gentleman soldier at the party.''

Ana's eyes almost popped out of her head. "A nice brat you are! I always said you'd come to no good. Your thieving has caused you to rob your own father. This is the de Porrez coat of arms.''

"My father?" gasped Martin. Could that handsome gentleman have been his father?

Ana no longer heard what Martin had to say. She tore open the fastening cords that tied the wallet together. She poured onto the table some thirty pieces of silver and gold. Martin, who had never before seen so much money, wondered what was happening. He noticed his mother was counting the money.

Then, looking up, she remarked curtly: "Tell me without lying how you robbed this man. If you don't, I'll whip you so you won't be able to walk for a week."

With dismay, Martin realized his mother distrusted him. She was convinced he had stolen the money. He put his hand into his pocket. He might as well give her everything. She'd find it sooner or later, anyway. "The same gentleman gave me this."

"A Rosary. . . a silver Rosary," laughed Ana. But as she took it in her hand, she trembled from head to foot.

"The gentleman told me he had carried it nine long years; that I'd probably put it to better use than he had. . ." Martin began to sob. Had not the kind gentleman said he could keep it? "Please let me at least keep the Rosary," he begged.

He saw his mother coming towards him. Instinctively he raised his arm in self-protection. His poor head had been whacked so often that he had learned it paid to stave off the blows. His head ached less when the thrashing was over.

"Martin. . . don't," said his mother remorsefully. She drew him towards her. She sat him on her lap as she wept over him.

He looked at his mother with surprise. His tears ceased in astonishment—the event was so unusual. Never before had he recalled seeing his mother shed a tear.

"It's mine," she said. "It's the Rosary I gave your father when we first met."

Her attitude had changed. There was something even kindly, motherly as they sat there—with Ana making Martin repeat word-for-word what had been said.

That night, indeed, was to be the turning point in Martin's life.

6
The Three R's

Doña Francisca had no intention of letting Don Juan forget his promise to the child. She made it quite clear that he had failed in his duty. In addition to neglecting the paternal instinct, which he had put aside, he was not acting like a nobleman of the de Porrez clan. He had tricked the mother into thinking there would be riches and honor; that her children would belong to the de Porrez family, who had fought so gallantly for Spain and conquered Granada. Instead, his children were barely kept alive by being fed refuse.

Don Juan refused to have an interview with the mother. Through Doña Francisca, he made arrangements for Martin to be taught to read and write. There was no suitable school in Lima which accepted a Negro child. The Spaniards looked down upon Negroes and Indians as inferior races—people to be utilized as servants and slaves, but not educated. Santiago had a qualified grammar school that made room for children of the poor. Don Juan arranged for Martin to go there to study.

When Don Juan left for Santiago—to return to his military post—he took Martin along. What a proud moment it was in the life of the lad! Newly outfitted, he took his place next to his dashing father. A group of cavaliers was making the journey together. Martin had become one of them.

The school in Santiago was heaven on earth to Martin. He had no worries as to where his next meal would come from. He had his regular hours of sleep. He was sheltered and cared for.

Don Juan had interviewed the headmaster. He took special pains to impress upon him the fact that, though he would pay for the child's tuition, legally he would not recognize Martin as his son.

Further, the instructors were to be warned that under no

circumstances was the boy to be pushed too far in his studies. He did not wish Martin to become a scholar. As the lad would acquire neither title nor money, he could never aspire to fame. He had merely taken a fancy to the bright, eager child. The boy wanted to read and write. With that accomplished, he would return to his mother and embark on the career of a day laborer or a miner. There was plenty of work to be found in Lima.

Martin had no time to be lonely. There was the novelty of the classroom, the art of mastering words, the handling of a pen — then, finally, writing. Martin was busy with his schooling. He wasted no time in setting himself to work. He easily mastered the three R's. For two blissful years, he plodded and acquired the rudiments of Spanish.

Don Juan de Porrez had fulfilled his New World missions so successfully that the Spanish Monarch wished to reward him. This time he assigned him to the duty of becoming Governor of Panama.

During the period that Martin was in town, Don Juan had forgotten about the boy. He was not in the least interested. Before his departure, however, he left funds for the support of both children with a relative. Enough money for Juana to provide her with a dowry when she became of marriageable age. For Martin, a fund which would enable him to complete his education. Since the boy's reports showed remarkable aptitude for studies, perhaps he might even aspire to the exalted position of becoming a clerk in some shop.

Martin felt secure in the knowledge that he was a burden to no one, that he could continue his beloved lessons uninterrupted. But Don Juan had barely sailed when Ana began to grow restless. She let the thought prey on her mind that money did not necessarily spell security. Martin was being temporarily provided for; but what about herself? Was it not better for the boy to be earning a living? She needed support. He could now assume that responsibility. The more she argued with herself, the more urgent appeared the necessity for withdrawing Martin from school. Selfishness and jealousy were the motives that prompted her action.

At the age of ten, Martin's schooling abruptly came to an end. Of course, the boy had no notion what had happened; nor did he realize why he was returning home. Sadly he bade farewell to his newly-made friends; to the professors whose affection he had won.

On reaching home, his mother informed him sarcastically that studies were a waste of time. Learning merely put queer, exalted notions into one's head. After all, he was a Negro. What was he trying to do—cramming himself with facts that would never be of use in later life? He was her son and she fully intended making him realize his obligation toward her. Suddenly it was as if the earth had opened and swallowed him. Secretly he had dreamt of becoming a doctor, of studying medicine. Now this hope, this ambition lay shattered.

Ana was going to send him off to the sugar cane plantation. A friend of hers was the overseer. He'd be just the right type to keep an eye on Martin. With lash in hand—he'd knock the studies out of his life. Besides, that way she'd be assured of a monthly stipend. There would be no further need to hope for benefactions from the hand of Don Juan de Porrez.

Once again Dõna Francisca came to the rescue. The heartbroken child had gone to her—bursting into tears as he bade her goodbye. Dõna Francisca was perturbed.

"Why, Martin. I heard you were proving yourself to be such an excellent scholar. How's this? Why are you going away? Why have you given up your studies?"

"It's none of my doing. I don't know. Mother merely keeps repeating that a nigger has no right to knowledge. She says work in the fields is meant for me. . . not poring over books and scribbling with a pen."

"In the name of heaven—what does your poor misinformed mother intend to do with you?"

"Tomorrow I leave for the sugar cane plantation. They need extra help. She says that's the work I'm best fitted for."

Dõna Francisca looked at the child kindly. "You liked your books. You loved your studies. What had you hoped to do if you had finished your schooling?"

Martin hung his head. He looked at her from the corner of his eye. He wondered if he dared confide in her his most prized secret.

"I have wanted. . . I hoped someday. . . to be a doctor like Doctor Velasco. He's poor, but he's always helping people. He was there when the old Indian woman died. It was he who wrapped her in my lovely new wool blanket. It was he who gave me medicine for the poor people on our street. He never charged anything for his services. He was always humming. . . always happy. . . always doing nice things."

Dõna Francisca drew the boy toward her. She put her arm around his trembling body. "Now don't be afraid. You're a brave little lad. I'll keep your secret. We'll tell no one. Someday when you are a great and famous doctor, perhaps you'll come to take care of me. Go to church and pray hard. Ask the sweet Madonna to help us. I have a plan. Say nothing of our conversation to anyone. Leave it to me. I'll see what I can do."

While Martin was praying in the Cathedral, kneeling before his favorite Madonna, he invoked her and all the saints in the litany with that faith which moves mountains.

Dõna Francisca had ordered her horse. She went to see her own surgeon. She explained the situation to the doctor. The child's life would be destroyed if given coarse work to do. He was never meant to be a day laborer. After a half hour of Doctor Ybarros' valuable time, his patient left him satisfied.

With dignity she climbed onto her waiting horse. She gave word that she wished to visit Dõna Velázquez. As she reined in her mount, the door opened.

Ana bowed in surprise. Of late, her visits had been less frequent. "Your Ladyship. . .what an honor. Won't you come in? The children are both here. In fact, Martin will be glad to see you. He's about to leave town for the sugar plantation."

"How nice. Is the boy going to have a well-deserved holiday?"

"Holiday?" frowned Ana. "My children will never have a holiday. We're too poor. No, he's grown up now. He's got to begin to earn a living."

"Why, how extraordinary," Dõna Francisca smiled. "I had intended talking to you about this long ago, but I felt that probably you wanted the boy to continue his studies. I've just been to see Doctor Ybarros—our most outstanding surgeon. He's my doctor as well. He's having difficulty getting a houseboy. He wants a youth who, in time, could become an apprentice. I spoke to him of Martin."

Ana's eyes sparkled with greed. Already she was counting the money that this would mean. Martin would be able to earn more in the household of a wealthy Peruvian doctor. She had no notion of letting the opportunity slip by.

"Do you think Martin would be eligible for the post? He's young and ignorant; but perhaps if Your Ladyship spoke in his favor, there might be an opening. I've trained him in the art of housekeeping. He's good at sweeping and making a fire. And as you personally know, in carrying out orders."

"Yes. I'm well aware of all these things," said Dõna Francisca, searching Martin's face intently. "Lad, what do you say? Do you think you'd like it?"

Martin's gaze looked as if he might have seen a vision. "I could try to please the doctor."

Dõna Francisca's visit resulted in a change in Ana's plans. An apprentice had to pay for the privilege of living in the household of a doctor. Acquiring the doctor's technique required years of learning. There were no medical universities or schools in those days.

Again Dõna Francisca had provided for Martin's lack of funds. Due to his poverty, there would be no expense. Besides, by helping in the household, he would earn a few silver pieces. This would pacify his mother's inordinate selfishness.

The day of the departure dawned. Bright and early, Ana had seen to it that Martin heated the copper cauldron. She poured the boiling water into the huge earthenware vessel which she used when doing the laundry. Martin was lathered, scoured and scrubbed. Not a part of his anatomy was spared. Not since he had been an infant had she bothered to bathe him. For Martin it was a humiliating

43

ordeal. Never before had his mother been concerned about his personal cleanliness. Now he was like a slippery eel.

His old clothes had been burned. Waiting was an almost brand-new suit given him by his father. Into this Martin wriggled. His straight black hair was well-greased and brushed, so that the stray locks were slick and tidy. Under his mother's eagle eye, Martin forced his feet into a pair of new shoes. Though many sizes too large, to the boy—accustomed to running about barefooted—the footwear cramped his toes.

Ana spent considerable time admonishing him how to act, what not to say. She warned him that the day he returned in disgrace, he'd be thrashed and sent to the country—never to return. His manner had always irritated her. He was so silent, so tight-lipped. If he would only weep or show some emotion. Even sullenness would have been preferable to his reproachful silence.

Martin carried with him all his earthly belongings tied in a shawl. Also the contract binding him as an apprentice to the household of Doctor Ybarros. Martin had read it. He had shown his mother where to sign her name, where to put the x-mark. Ana could neither read nor write. As the mother of a minor, she had thus legally given her consent to an apprenticeship that would require years of hard work and study.

The doctor lived at the other end of town. The noonday sun with its scorching heat beat down on the broad-brimmed palm hat. Beads of perspiration stood in great drops on his forehead. He trudged along laboriously in his huge boots. It was the siesta hour. Still he kept on going. Finally, no longer able to stand the anguish of blistered feet, Martin loosened the laces and tied them together. He slung his shoes across his back.

Though Martin was brave, still he was afraid. What if the doctor changed his mind? Had he been told the truth about this youth? He felt he would never have the strength or courage to face his mother again. She had no love in her heart for him.

Fearful, Martin continued on his way. He traversed the Plaza de Armas. As he came to the door of his beloved Cathedral, he had no time to go within. Bareheaded he gazed at the beautiful facade.

There above the main entrance towered the Madonna. Her hands were folded as in a benediction. He crossed himself reverently and said a fervent prayer, asking her to help him; then continued on his way.

As the gaunt, yellowish Cathedral was left behind him, Martin gained courage. He whistled a merry tune so as not to think. Thoughts were frightening.

7
The Doctor's Apprentice

After much reflection, Martin decided he could not be wrong. He stood undecided before a Spanish colonial residence. He'd never seen anything so beautiful. He'd hesitated because surely doctors did not live in palaces. Had he known anything about architecture, he would have noticed the influence of Moorish sculpture and filigree. Most of Martin's youth had been spent in squalid sections of the city. Naturally, he was abashed.

Finally he summoned sufficient courage to take the initial step. With heart beating so loudly anyone could have heard it, he clutched the bell. It clanged resoundingly. When a liveried servant swung open the massive doors, Martin wanted to run. Instead, he followed timidly. There was a long, cool, dark corridor. The brightness of the sun on the scorched road had blinded him. Light shone dimly in the distance. They passed through a colonnade that bordered the gaily planted patio.

Martin was shown to a waiting room. The doctor was out. The receptionist expected him. Would Martin wait? He studied the magnificent ceiling of black carved wood, went into raptures over massive folios. He peered out of the window into the patio with its hanging plants, its countless palms. In one corner of the shaded gallery, servants chattered as they spun the silky wool of the alpaca.

Suddenly he was conscious of the coolness of the marble floor. He looked down, saw his dusty feet. Chagrined by his stupidity, he undid the knots hurriedly. He'd been so busy hoping to get into his shoes before being detected that he'd not heard the door open, had not heard anyone approach.

A kindly voice, half-chuckling, exclaimed: "Well. . . well I never. So this is what Doña Francisca sends me for an assistant?"

Feeling the friendly hand on his shoulder, Martin was startled but not afraid. "I'm sorry, Sir. I forgot my shoes," he said.

"Can't blame you, lad. I'd be doing the same if my wife were not always meddling in my affairs. Stand up and let me look at you."

Martin did as he was told. "Won't I do? Please let me try."

"It's not that you won't do. It's your size that's against you, boy. You can't be strong. The work is hard, the hours long."

"Sir, if you let me try—you'll find I'm as strong as a llama."

The doctor shook his head, rubbing his white beard in a perplexed manner. "I can't understand what's taken possession of Doña Francisca. She was as persistent as a mule. I hate to disappoint her since she's my best client. In fact, she keeps me busy minding her charity cases. But, look. . . child. You go back and tell Doña Francisca you've changed your mind."

"But I have not," pleaded Martin.

"See here. After all, this is not a nursery. Morning, noon and night I'm at the service of others. Sickness and death are not pretty sights. You're too young to face their grim horror. Better go back to your mother. That's where you belong."

Trembling, Martin pulled out the contract. "I beg your pardon, Sir. But mother has signed the contract. It's a ten-year one. I'm twelve now. After ten years under your care, I'll be twenty-two. You'll find me willing to learn. I love the poor and sick. There is not a Negro or Indian who's died on our street whom I have not helped. I'm not afraid of either death or suffering. I've seen so much that I want to help."

"No, son. I understand how you feel. Doña Francisca told me about your unhappy home, your selfish mother. It's a pity you've walked this long, hot road. I'm too old to waste time teaching an infant."

Martin remembered that before medicine and surgery came haircutting. The profession of a barber was linked to a medical career. Doña Francisca had reminded him that the doctor maintained his barber shop in town, where he also kept his apothecary.

"I'm really older than I look. Perhaps you'll let me start as an errand boy. Won't you let me try? When I get back, I'll sweep the floor. There is always a lot of hair to brush away. I'm good at sharpening knives. Your razor blade will never be dull. When there's an operation, I'll mop up the blood and strew the floor with clean white sand." Martin pointed to the ceiling. "See the cobwebs? I can climb up there and dust them out of sight."

The doctor laughed. "You're a persuasive young fellow with plenty of grit. Most people are scared to death of me. Here you stand—pleading—as if your life depended on a fair trial."

"I'm afraid it does. If you don't accept me, I'm off tomorrow to the sugar plantation. They'll put me to work cutting cane. It would break my heart. I don't mind how hard I work, or how many hours. Just as long as I can be near the medicine chest and help relieve pain."

"A plucky lad. . . that's what you are. I haven't the heart to turn you down. I know I'm a fool. Common sense tells me you'll not last a week. But, come. Give me the contract. We'll begin right now."

Martin's eyes almost popped out of his head. He'd come so near to losing what he had hoped for that the excitement was almost too much.

"Thank you, Sir. Thank you." He seized the hand of the doctor and held it gratefully. "I'll do all I can."

Under propitious auspices, Martin's medical career started. The training was slow and long. Unscrupulous pretenders hung up their signs. Life meant nothing to them. They were totally unconcerned about either furthering it or alleviating pain. They were out for money. The result was that the few good doctors in Lima had no rest.

At first, Martin wielded the huge, fan-shaped feather duster. He waged incessant war on both cobwebs and dust. Soon the master entrusted to his care the sharp scissors used to cut moustaches or to trim beards. The boy had a steady hand. Patrons liked the lad. Martin became a professional, using a footstool to reach his customers.

Martin followed the doctor about like a watchdog. Not a movement or change of expression passed unobserved. He carried the doctor's medical kit. One day, when requiring an assistant, the doctor called on Martin. He was astonished to find that Martin had foreseen his wishes. The sharp knife needed to lance the boil was ready. He knew what was required to cauterize wounds.

Unflinching, the child stood strong—ministering to the suffering. It was he who held the feverish limb. It was he who remained motionless while the knife was thrust deep into a blood vessel. Nor did he falter at the sight of profuse bleeding. He realized it was the only sure method for lowering the high temperature of those parched with fever. For milder cases, leeches were used. Again, it was Martin who handled the loathsome creatures about to burst after a gory meal.

He learned a thousand useful things. All of these he put into constant practice. Soon he was just as efficient with herbs as he was with the knife. He worked during the long hours of the night, studying and concocting new methods for alleviating smarting pain; for calming the horrors of delirium. With one good pull, he could extricate the aching tooth. He was quick in stopping the flow of blood. Broken bones were set and put into splints. Merciful time would heal them.

Days were spent trudging the dusty, narrow Lima lanes. He had progressed so rapidly that Doctor Ybarros had freed him from his contract and the obligations of serving a ten-year apprenticeship. Martin had matured so quickly that he was considered one of the great rising lights in the medical world. Yet Martin fled from the rich. He felt they could depend on their money for immediate help. The poor had no one. He rarely accepted pay.

Martin needed medicines. He had to have a well-stocked apothecary if he wished to relieve ailments. From the Inca Indians he had learned much. He had helped them. He brought their babies into the world. He had saved them from death. They, in turn, imparted to him the secrets of age-old remedies. They taught him how to strip the bark off the *cinchona* tree. Not only did quinine serve as an excellent tonic, but this bitterest of all medicines was the surest remedy for malarial afflictions.

In another jar, he stored leaves from the *coca* shrub. This made soothing poultices and had the effect of a local anesthetic. Oil in which the *coca* leaves had been pounded was an indispensable balm that relieved inflammation and pain. *Cocaine* was used as a tonic, even as a drug.

On through the night—with his great marble mortar and stone pestle—Martin pounded and formulated his medicines. He gathered medicinal mushrooms. He dug for roots, grinding them as he did ginger.

By dawn he rose to work in his garden of herbs. He loved the early hours of the day when he dug and contemplated in his medicinal garden. There he planted and toiled, working with his plants, shrubs and trees. His enclosed garden became a laboratory to impart relief to pain-wracked bodies.

The *camomile* was plentiful. This stringent, scented herb of the aster family was prolific. Martin hired gamins from the street to pick its daisy-shaped flowers. When brewed, it made a fragrant tea used to dispel colic. *Cassia* bushes grew into trees. The *senna* leaves were dried. Their purgative properties made them invaluable. There, too, he raised his blood-drawing leeches. For, nothing was overlooked by Martin in his insatiable desire to alleviate suffering.

Martin had become a jack-of-all-trades. His resourcefulness brought him patients from all classes—the rich as well as mendicants. The young apprentice truly became all things to all men. He was physician, surgeon, family consultant and chemist. He was the most outstanding diagnostician of all South America. People traveled all the way from Mexico for consultations. With remarkable ability, this young doctor handled the most difficult situations.

He had always been intolerant of pain. It hurt him to see others suffer. Probably that was the secret of his success—his longing to be of service to humanity. Pain created in him a fierce desire to fight it, to overcome it.

At such times his usual shyness vanished. Quick, sharp-eyed, his deft fingers skillfully felt what was wrong. His keen straightforwardness restored lost confidence. Doctor Martin de Porrez was a fighter. He fought death so effectively that, ultimately, he was the victor. His patients survived when others had already mourned them as dead.

The only time this young doctor's feelings were hurt was when he was offered remuneration. Those great, dark-brown eyes of his would look sadly at the outstretched hand. Shaking his head, he would remark:

"Don't you know that healing is a gift of God? Please don't pay me for my services. I have done this gladly to help you. But, instead, you may give to the poor — who are less fortunate than you are — what you've set aside for me."

8
Renunciation

Doctor Martin de Porrez lived in a period of depression. Barely fifty years before his birth, the Conqueror Pizarro and his conquistadores had destroyed the great Inca Civilization. Then had come the frenzied rush for gold. Though Lima still remained the dominant Spanish city in the New World, its people knew what suffering meant.

In Peru there was no middle class. There were the fabulously wealthy and the desperately poor. The aftermath of success, with its orgy of spending and riotous living, had proved to be poverty. People died of starvation in a land of plenty. The rich were unconcerned about the poor. They were a cruel, heartless lot —most of them bent on their own pleasures.

Doctor de Porrez had inherited from his mother the cheerful characteristics of the Negro race; their peace-loving and generous spirit. From his father he had acquired innate tact and statesmanship. He had a remarkable power of organization; the persevering zeal and energy for which the Spaniards were so outstanding. With these qualities, it was natural that he be popular with people of all nationalities and loved by those of every race and creed.

Had he inherited great riches, he would have spent his last *centavo* on others. Nothing was ever used for his own personal needs or gain. He was selfless, giving lavishly of both his time and talent. His insatiable desire to·serve was never satisfied. He was ever busily engaged in curing the ills of others with never a thought for himself. As a result, he was always insufficiently clothed and hard-pressed for time.

Day after day, year after year, the narrow thoroughfare on which he lived became impassable. It was lined by a motley crowd of rich and poor, elbowing its way to the doctor's office. Strange as it was in a land where little concern or regard was shown the Negro, a Negro doctor could and did command the admiration and respect of all.

Representatives of the Spanish Crown called him friend. Governors asked his advice. Archbishops and Bishops were grateful if he could spare them a few moments. The sick, the poor, the halt, the blind came to him to be cured. He helped all—never discriminating. By his largesse, by his humanity, Martin did more than any other person of his time to overcome racial prejudice.

Though his fame was to make him renowed throughout South America, success never turned Martin's head. He was convinced that God was using him as a channel through which to distribute the gift of healing. He felt it was as supernatural a gift as was faith. Lives that had been despaired of came back from the very jaws of death. All that he had done was to pray over the inanimate object that lay there. He'd made the Sign of the Cross — that sign which has power over life and death, over good and evil. There could be no scientific explanation. It was a miracle of faith, implicit faith in God.

Martin was afraid of publicity. He shunned it as he did sin. He also realized there would be those who wanted the sensational. There would always be a flock of sentimentalists who craved something to rave about. These Martin loathed. He was shrewd. His insight into human nature prevented this type of a following.

To cloak this gift of healing, which he could often impart with the mere laying of his hands upon the patient, he picked out more natural means. He always carried with him his medicines. When medical science was at a standstill, it was then that he ordered the contents of a bottle to be taken at specific hours. Martin had prayed. His faith had brought about the healing; not the medicine, which had been well water.

Again, when unable to travel so as to reach a dying patient in time, like the saints before him, he sent the gift of a new nightgown or a fragrant bunch of rosemary. The results were the same: life, health, healing.

Martin's spirituality was so outstanding because he was so silent. There was no outward demonstration, no ecstatic outburst. His mysticism was kept to himself. He loved his neighbor far more than his own person. He loved God ardently and served his fellow man with such affection because he saw in man a reflection of his Maker. Martin was never to write any treatises or leave behind him voluminous confessions. Very little that Martin said has been preserved through the centuries.

When Martin first started the practice of medicine, he had managed to snatch a few hours for rest. These, supposedly set aside for sleep, were devoted to contemplation. His quarters were in a tiny room in the attic of a miserable boardinghouse. Year by year, as his success grew, the greater became his need for quiet contemplation. The leisure hours of the night were spent in prayer. When dawn crept over the sleeping city, Martin was lost in meditation.

Martin was hard on himself. Often he severely chastised his body. The old landlady was puzzled by her strange boarder. He never went out to parties. He rarely had any visitors. She wondered how he could possibly burn so many of her candles.

Every morning the supply given him the night before was burnt out. He used more in one night than did all the other boarders.

Not wanting to hurt his feelings by appearing to be curious, she decided personally to investigate the cause for this waste. She sneaked up the creaking stairs and peered through the cracks in the door. Yes, there was the light of the candle. To her horror—she saw Martin inflicting the scourge upon his bared shoulders. The silence of the night was broken by the sound of the whip.

Having taken his penance, the unsuspecting Martin fell on his knees. There, before a statue of the Madonna — Our Lady, Queen of the Most Holy Rosary — he knelt immovable. His face was bathed in tears. His body was wreathed in light. So dazzling was the light that the old lady was ashamed. Never again was she to doubt the use to which the candles were put. Her humble and unobstrusive boarder could burn as many as he wished.

Womanlike, the landlady ceaselessly wagged her tongue about the remarkable virtues of the Negro doctor. Soon all Lima learned that, when not curing ailing bodies, he was praying.

Martin had made a point of seeking seclusion when he communed with God. The rush and bustle of daily life, with its exacting demands, exhausted him spiritually. He was constantly struggling within himself. Had not God made him to know Him, to love Him and to serve Him in this world? Yet he was devoting more time to man, less to God.

He felt he would have to put a stop to this. He became obsessed with the thought that he had crowded God out of his life. He, Martin, had permitted material things to permeate his life to the extent that the spiritual side had become lopsided.

Living as he did, he realized it was utterly impossible for him to divide his day into periods of prayer and work. There was only one alternative — the cloister. Religious life would help him find true balance. There would no longer be the importunity of suffering humanity whom he could not bear to turn away. He would renounce his medical career and embrace a life of prayer and contemplation.

Martin was not running away from work. He loved his profession. But the turning point had come. The crossroads met as they do in all great lives. He had to make up his mind. No one could do it for him.

After serious deliberation, Martin — who had such tremendous devotion to Our Lady of the Most Holy Rosary — wished to consecrate his life in an order where the Rosary was honored. Martin, who in spite of success always remained humble and shy, now found it difficult to take the initial step. Summoning his courage, he rang the bell of the Convent of the Holy Rosary. He asked for an interview with Father Provincial.

Father Juan de Lorenzana was Dominican Provincial in Peru. He was one of those haughty Spaniards who sized up his subjects according to their rank in the nobility. Though in the eyes of the church, Peru was definitely considered a missionary country still in the process of being evangelized, a spirit of worldliness had crept into the order. Its primitive spirit — that original fervor endowed to it by its saintly founder, Dominic—had been somewhat clouded.

Every Spanish family wanted the honor of having a son in holy orders. If not pursuing a military career in the service of His Majesty — then a son in the priesthood, enjoying the benefits of a well-endowed cathedral; or devoting his life to God in some religious community. Unfortunately, there was great abuse. Instead of sifting and weeding in their choice of worthy subjects, superiors permitted a mercenary spirit to guide them. Monasteries had to sustain themselves. After all, monks could not subsist "on bread alone."

Naturally, Father Provincial was not at all anxious to admit a Negro. He had no intention of displeasing the difficult members of his community. There was a faction of recalcitrants—the diehards who openly rebelled at being moulded into first-rate Dominicans. He well knew how every convent had its problem vocations. There were the very young: promising subjects whom one always hoped to reform. There were the old to whom second childhood brought a reoccurrence of faults long past buried under the weight of years: sometimes a slight infraction of the rule; an infidelity to grace; or other temptation.

The Superior's hands were tied. He had his own problems. Certainly it would be folly to create an incident by accepting this Negro.

Sensing Father Provincial's haughty coldness, Martin fell to his knees. "I humbly beg of you to accept me within the Dominican Order."

Father Juan de Lorenzana looked at the kneeling figure. "I fear you are too old. Besides, you have years of a successful medical career behind you. You see, we have an age limit."

"True, I have behind me a long career. I started young. I'm only twenty-four now. But success and honors have not turned my head."

"You have never had Latin. There would be obstacles to your studying for the priesthood."

Poor Martin gasped. "Oh. . . such a thought never entered my head. I have no lofty aspiration for either the priesthood or becoming a lay brother. I merely ask leave to join the third order. As a tertiary I would have the privilege of sharing the innumerable benefits derived from being united with the Order of Saint Dominic. If you accept me, I would gladly come in the capacity of a servant."

"Do you realize what that means?" asked the Provincial quietly.

"Yes, I think I do. It means waiting on others and being given chores that one would hesitate to ask someone to perform."

"That's right. The most menial, the most humble duties would fall to you. Don't forget that all your life you've been independent. You've come and gone as you pleased. You'll find it doubly difficult to submit to obedience every moment of the day. You'd no longer be a free agent. You'd be told what to do and expected to carry out orders as if you were a soldier in the King's Army."

"No," said Martin. "This thought does not frighten me. If I come, I do so because I wish to serve God by taking vows of poverty, chastity and obedience."

"There is one great difficulty which neither of us has considered. We might as well face it. That's racial prejudice."

Martin smiled. "I was disowned by a white father, a Spanish

nobleman, because of my dusky color. All my life I have seen the horrors and suffering inflicted by those biased with this hatred in their hearts. I faced this menace in the world in which I lived; and, by the grace of God, overcame it. Surely in religious life the problems will not be as great. After all, I have no right to expect anything. I'm really a mulatto. I'll take the consequences."

Father Provincial was moved. After sensing Martin's deep spirituality and humility, he hardly felt like banging the door in his face. He'd make it easier by backing out of it gracefully.

"So important a decision is not up to me. I will present it to the council when they next meet. We will let you know what decision has been reached."

As Martin was about to leave the convent, he said: "I have implicit faith in the Madonna—Our Lady, Queen of the Holy Rosary. She will see to it that you change your mind. The next time I see you, you'll tell me I'm admitted."

9
All Things To All Men

The world in general was always most unconcerned when anyone entered the convent. The nearest kith and kin; or, perhaps a few friends, might be glad or sorry. But with Martin it was a very different story. A strange rumor persisted. The Negro doctor intended renouncing his practice. He was going to become a servant in the great Dominican Convent.

The poor were in an uproar. They tried to reach Martin. He had already gone. Rumor had it that their beloved physician had been given the lowest rank in the order. To climax the gossip, Doctor de Porrez had been seen working with the slaves. He was doing manual labor: carting manure, sweeping out stables. In fact, tending to work that was reserved for the lowest ebb of humanity. For the Spaniards had a caste system.

At this auspicious moment, the Governor of Panama happened to arrive in Lima on a business trip. He was immediately approached and questioned as to the intentions of his son.

Naturally, Martin had not informed his father of his intended move. They had not corresponded for years. In fact, His Excellency had no interest whatsoever in the activities of the doctor. He had been somewhat irritated by the fame and publicity acquired by Martin. He definitely felt that Negroes and Indians had to be kept in their place.

He highly disapproved of such gentlemen as the Archbishop of Mexico and the governors of various cities traveling all the way to Lima for a diagnosis by a Negro physician. He confessed that things would have been very different if Martin had had other traits. Thus Governor de Porrez had remained unconcerned as to what Martin did.

Everyone rushed to His Excellency, asking him if he had heard the latest news. He fully expected some sort of scandal. Instead, he learned that his offspring had entered the Convent of the Holy Rosary; not as a priest; not as a lay brother — but as a tertiary servant.

The Governor was filled with rage. This was an aspersion on the honor of the de Porrez family. Was he not Governor of Panama? Had he not had a successful military career in the service of the Spanish Crown? He'd teach that good-for-nothing prior a sound lesson for degrading his son. In this mood he stalked to the convent.

The two haughty Spaniards met. The Governor of Panama and the very decided Dominican Provincial confronted each other. Father Juan de Lorenzana explained that it was out of the question for a Negro to study for holy orders. Don Juan raged. He would report this appalling affront to the Spanish Crown. After all, a man bearing the de Porrez name was entitled to consideration. What did it matter if he were a mulatto? He was entitled to the honors of the priesthood.

All the while, Martin was unaware that his father was in the house. Had he known, he would have prevented the visit. Position and rank meant nothing to Martin. He was quite contented with his humble station. It was what he had asked for. It was what had been given him. He had no further aspirations.

As neither the Provincial nor the Governor could reach a satisfactory conclusion, Martin was sent for. No one could have been more surprised on reaching the parlor than Martin. Dismayed that he was the cause of a conflict, he tried to prevail upon his father to drop the matter. He hoped Father Provincial was not too annoyed. He really had had no say in the matter. He had no ambitions to be a priest.

The Governor shouted: "What! Now that you have a chance to secure a dispensation to study for the presthood?" Then he added determinedly: "I'll attend to everything. I have always had my way before. I'll certainly have it now."

"Thank you, father. But it would be a waste of time. Even if the honor were forced on me, I would never consent. I will never change my mind."

"Boy, are you crazy? Do you intend to let them kick you around as if you were a nobody?"

"Why. . . that's exactly what I am. Why should I pretend to be somebody? I came here for seclusion and I found it. I wanted to lead a life of solitude and prayer. I have tasted honor and success. These I've left behind."

The Provincial interrupted "Your son sought admission, asking for the lowest position. Is that not so, Martin?"

"Yes. It was I who asked for the position I hold. Now that I have it — I wish to keep it, thank you."

"You forget you're my son. If you had not had the misfortune to be as dark as you are, you would be heir to all my estates. After all, I can't permit you to drag my name in the mud."

Martin was very sad. "Father, isn't it now a bit late in life to acknowledge me openly as your child? There was a time when I needed your friendship, your help. But you had no use either for me or for my long-suffering mother. You need not fear. Your name will never be tarnished by me. Here I am already known as Brother Martin. For the rest of my life, I hope that as Brother

Martin I can serve God and my fellow man.''

Father Provincial was profoundly struck by Martin's sincerity. He could make no mistake by admitting him within the congregation. To pacify the irate Governor, he would permit him to receive the habit of a lay brother. He felt, after what he had seen and heard, that he was taking a good risk.

He was sure to face local displeasure, when he told the brethren that he had accepted Martin. They might make it exceedingly difficult for Martin, but his word was law. He was convinced that Martin had the stern stuff it takes to make a good religious. Though proud, the Provincial was also gifted with a sense of humor. He chuckled when he realized the stir in chapter his announcement would make.

Brother Martin went through a rigorous and austere period of training. He was spared nothing. He was given the most menial duties. He was still in charge of the stables. Every morning after the conventual Mass, there was the washroom that had to be scrubbed, the corridors to be swept. In the afternoon during the siesta hour, Martin had to clean the kitchen floor, polish the hot stove and empty the ashes.

No matter how difficult his tasks, his faith and courage remained unperturbed. To a man who had been doing brain work, this was stultifying. But Martin turned everything into a game. He was happy, although constantly humiliated; happy because the cloud of doubt and uncertainty as to his conduct had lifted. He was convinced he was doing God's will; that he had been destined to serve within the cloister.

Things certainly had changed in his life. The unfair, bigoted resentment of the religious hurt him. They were very different from the people he had left. Martin had just cause for complaint. Yet he was the last person who would have thought of putting into words what he endured. It was part of the life he had embraced.

The priests whom he served, the lay brothers under whom he worked constantly rebuffed him. Few in passing him along the corridors even returned his smile. Martin had known what to expect in a sin-ridden world. But he was taken aback by what he now endured. He was the last one to demand anything. He knew he had been born in humble circumstances. Because of his color he had been an outcast.

His medical profession had enabled him to establish himself on a different footing. The world had needed him. It had come to him for service. Unstintingly he had rendered it to the best of his ability.

Some of the brethren treated him exactly as if he were a slave. Others snickered. When no one was around, they called him "galley bird" — or, more often, "you dog of a mulatto." Some waited till he was within hearing. Then they made sarcastic remarks about the "nigger doctor."

Martin bore the brunt of the storm. He continued his strenuous work as if he had been born deaf and blind. But, inwardly, he suffered. He rebelled. He was human and longed for sympathy and understanding. He realized he would hardly find it amongst the members of the community. Thus all the more he was thrown towards God.

As a child, when forsaken by his mother, he had turned to prayer. He had then acquired the art of contemplation, the ability of withdrawing to the inner sanctuary of the soul. He had learned how to talk to God. Instead of rehearsing to himself what he had heard, what had been said, what had been done, he dropped these disturbing factors of his daily life. He conversed with God. Absorbed in God's beauty, His magnificence, His Love — Martin was drawn to a higher sphere. His earthly troubles vanished.

Many were the humiliations that Martin endured. In later years — after he had won the love and esteem of his companions — it was they, themselves, who told of their cruelty.

Sadly they recounted how they went out of their way to inflict pain on Brother Martin. Their pride, their ego had been hurt. They resented the very thought that a "nigger" should share their beautiful convent. They felt he had no right to be treated as an equal. In chapter, they took delight in humiliating him in public. They were constantly faultfinding. He had forced himself on them. They would make his life so miserable that he would gladly renounce his religious aspirations.

Somehow, they had not counted on his spirit of perseverance. Their quarrels were always one-sided. A lopsided fight has no zest, usually dying a natural death. Since it required two to pick a quarrel, it was they who invariably lost.

Instead of lessening, the trials grew more severe. Certainly there was no letup. His companions hated him. Why, they did not know, except that bigotry had biased their opinion.

Fortunately, Martin's superiors were of a different caliber. They had watched. They had seen him bear excruciating criticism. They felt his testing and proving period had been severe enough. He had endured the primary examinations. He was now eligible for a position of trust.

The infirmary was poorly run. In the one convent, there were over three hundred religious. Besides, there were a goodly number of servants and slaves who worked on the land. Brother Martin was named Head Infirmarian.

Martin was overcome with joy. Nothing could have pleased him more. Here was a double opportunity. He could continue serving God while serving his fellow man. He had missed the sick. Now he could put his former knowledge to use. For a time, it had almost appeared as if he'd never again handle instruments or his beloved medicines.

The spirit in the community was hostile. They had had to endure a Negro in their midst. Now the sick and infirm would be at his mercy! They were loud in their protest and denunciation.

Brother Martin learned much within the Convent of the Holy Rosary. He found that most of the brethren were very human. Their frailties were many and great. As infirmarian, his patients were most exacting. They had no respect for him. They refused to carry out his orders. They were haughty, proud, demanding. Even his wealthiest clients had been easier to satisfy.

Amongst the members of this large community were the mediocre; the difficult characters whom superiors tolerated. They felt obliged to overlook their idiosyncrasies. These lukewarm religious were the bane of the community. These were the ones who turned Martin's early religious life into a veritable martyrdom. These were the patients of whom attendants were most terrified when assigned to nurse them. They would plead that Brother Martin come to their rescue. Would he see what he could do? His tact, his statesmanship pacified the irked spirits.

On one certain occasion, Father Prior was making the rounds of the infirmary. He was gravely concerned. The silence of the infirmary was broken by shrieking. Fearful that one of the patients had taken a turn for the worse, he went from door to door, trying to locate the sick person whom he was certain was raving and delirious.

Aghast, he heard the coarse shouts: "You imposter! You've kept me waiting. You good-for-nothing, lazy nigger. . . what do you take me for? I'll teach you, you dog of a mulatto. . ."

Concluding that the patient had gone out of his right mind, silently Father Prior entered the room. Propped up in bed sat the very man Father Prior expected to find delirious; while kneeling on the floor, head prostrate on the ground, lay Brother Infirmarian.

Annoyed, the superior demanded: "How can you forget yourself like this? How dare you talk to a member of our community in the tone you have used? You are a disgrace to your vocation."

Then, summoning Brother Martin to the corridor, he expostulated: "Why did you permit this? He's not even delirious. You should have stopped him from addressing you in such an unbecoming manner."

Martin smiled sheepishly. "I could not help it. I knew that he had merely lost his temper. He often gets these tantrums. This time, I felt within me such a surge of revolt and indignation, that — to prevent myself from answering back — I fell on my face. This gave me time to gain mastery over my wounded pride. Even though it's not yet Lent, I was receiving an extra sprinkling of ashes on my poor, unworthy head."

"Yes. . . yes, I see," replied Father Prior, deeply moved. "But I'll make sure that this doesn't happen again. I'll have someone else nurse him. He does not deserve your care or attention. He'll never have another opportunity to humiliate you."

Martin looked hurt. "As a special favor, won't you permit to stay on the case? I'd like to handle this irritable priest for a little while longer."

Martin had his way. Not many days elapsed before Father Antonio had reformed his ways, mended his nasty temper.

On another occasion, Martin had been seen kneeling and kissing the foot of another of his patients. Asked why he had acted thus, Martin gave a very simple explanation.

"It's a Spanish custom to kiss the hand of a priest. In this case, I felt unworthy to kiss his hand. Instead I knelt and kissed his foot."

His superior suspected there was more to this tale. He inquired and learned from the priest that he had roundly reprimanded Martin, talking to him sharply and curtly. Martin, instead of greeting him as was customary, had kissed his foot.

There was a priest dying of pleurisy. Knowing that his last hour had come, he sent for Martin. When the two were alone, he whispered: "Take your hand. Place it here where the pain is unbearable." Martin did as he was told.

Father Louis de Guadelupe pleaded: "Brother Martin — pray. . . pray." Instantly the pain left. The priest was cured.

At the same time, in another section of the infirmary, lay a great, strong man who had never been sick in his life. Father Pedro de Montesdosci had met with an accident. He had injured his right leg. Infection and blood poisoning had set in. Martin was unsuccessful in his remedies. A consultation with several leading surgeons confirmed his fears. Amputation was necessary in order to save the priest's life.

Father Prior came in person to break the news. He wished to encourage him to bear bravely the trial awaiting him. The poor man was suffering excruciating torments. There were no remedies to alleviate the torturing pain. He was so upset by the doctor's verdict that he stormed and raged. His temper was so violent that the prior left in fear and trembling.

Father Pedro blamed God for his ills; upbraided those around him for the frightful misfortune which was about to befall him. At times, the poor man was delirious. Martin never left his side.

On one such occasion, he heard the priest express a wish for his favorite dish. It was something that long ago he had enjoyed at home. Brother Martin realized how severely the patient must be suffering from the gangrenous infection. He walked to town, procuring the coveted viand at the market. When he returned to the convent, he personally supervised the preparation of this special dish.

Triumphantly he carried the tray to the sickroom. "See what I have brought you! It's something you've been wanting."

Father Pedro was curious. "What is it?" he asked. "Nothing tastes good any more. I can guess what it is with my eyes closed."

Brother Martin laughed. "I think your surprise will be complete."

Father Pedro was so deeply touched by Martin's sympathetic understanding, that — with tears in his eyes — he caught hold of Martin's hand. "How can I thank you? You're always doing the unexpected."

Then, not only did the patient clean his plate; but his former jovial spirits returned. Martin had brought him back to his senses. He realized he was not abandoned; that there were people about who cared.

"Come. . . Brother Martin," he pleaded. "Kneel by my bed and pray for me. Ask God if it be His holy will that I be cured. I dread an operation. What will I ever do, hobbling around on one leg?"

Martin knelt long and prayed hard. He placed both his hands on the burning, tormented limb. The patient felt better, much better. When the surgeon arrived to perform the amputation, he almost had a stroke. Father Pedro was walking! Within a few days, the wound was entirely healed. Father Pedro was cured. Brother Martin had worked another of his miracles.

Many of the young novices were handling carpentry tools for the first time. Often there were serious accidents. Brother Martin frequently was called upon to perform first aid. One of the most serious cases was that of a young novice. The lad had nearly cut off two fingers with a sharp knife. By the time Martin got the case, the arm was badly inflamed. It was too late to stop the infection.

Brother Martin, sensing the novice's fright, tried to reassure him. "Be not afraid, my dear child. You'll not be sent back to the world you have forsaken. The Master, who holds in the palm of His hands both life and death, will care for you. He will cure you of your wound — even though it is a dangerous one."

Then, taking from his pocket some herbs, he made a poultice. This he laid on the fingers. After saying a few short prayers and blessing the lad, he left the novitiate to return to the infirmary. The next day, the novice could use his hand. The inflammation had gone.

The miracles Martin performed could fill a book. His works of mercy were as numerous. In a short time, he was as busy as he had been in the world. Night and day, he was healing bodies. Often he healed the spirit as well. His silence, his humility, his kindliness were sermons in themselves. Soon the very ones who had been the loudest in their disdain called on him. He was indispensable.

Naturally, there were always a few who were jealous. They considered him an idiot. Martin merely shrugged his shoulders and smiled to himself. He exused them by saying: "How can it be otherwise? Naturally, they think I'm an escaped slave."

Though Martin was Head Infirmarian, he always reserved unto himself some of the more menial duties. In those days it was considered debasing to do manual labor. No lay brother would have been asked to sweep a corridor. This duty was set aside for the slaves. Martin permitted no slaves to sweep his infirmary corridors. He never looked on any form of labor as debasing. Even after the fame of his cures spread within the convent, there were still jibes thrust at him. He had merely to wield his broom to start a fresh flow of criticism.

On one such occasion, a priest remarked sarcastically: "Brother. . . you have no right to be in our convent, disturbing our peace. You should be placed in a penitentiary."

Before the astonished priest could finish his sentence, he saw Martin — broom in hand — on his knees. "You're perfectly right. I know I am, indeed, the most miserable of God's creatures —

unworthy of the honor of being here. If you would kindly make known to me my faults, I will try to correct and overcome them.''

Several others witnessed this scene, though at the time neither Martin nor the priest knew they were being watched. It was said that, from then on, that priest never again reprimanded Martin or made sarcastic remarks.

Others, too, began to be a little more watchful of their criticism. Martin was too humble. Each time it was their pride that showed up.

10
Lima's Humanitarian

To keep track of all that Martin did would be humanly impossible. The story of Brother Martin provides passing sketches of one who lived in the 16th century — a very full life about which only a few salient factors are known.

Within this convent, he not only was Head Infirmarian; he was doctor and barber as well. As guardian of the linen room, he had a tremendous task. Though others worked under him, his was the responsibility. He also was in charge of the garden, where he spent a number of hours daily. Though this was an innovation, his superiors hoped that by his example he might bring about a change of heart in the brethren.

Since the Spanish Conquest, no white man had touched the soil. This was considered the job of slaves. No matter how poor, people preferred starvation to losing caste. The result was that much valuable land went to waste. Martin, who was completely indifferent to public opinion, gladly tilled, plowed and harvested.

During the long hours of the night, he rarely rested. No one ever heard him as he glided about noiselessly. Wherever he was most needed—there he would be. No one learned how he found out. Was it intuition or was it miraculous? Martin would stand by the bedside with a sleeping potion. Or, perhaps, a poultice or a soothing drink.

The sick were locked into their rooms by the infirmarian on night duty. Malaria, with its appalling delirium, was so prevalent that it was considered safest to keep the patients confined. Brother Martin — with fingers to his lips — stood there smiling. He would change the drenched linens, administer leeches, massage with ointments. He had come to alleviate pain.

He refused to answer the question of how he had come. Usually it was in answer to a prayer; a cry for help to endure the unbearable agony. The door remained bolted and locked. Weird as it seems, he disappeared in the same manner.

The next morning, the patients he had visited in this strange way were usually cured. In other cases there was a pronounced change for the better.

Sometimes Father Prior asked Martin to keep watch through the night. Quietly he would enter the room. He would squat on the ground. When asked why he would not use a chair, he remarked: "The earth is plenty good enough for me."

Numerous details were handed down, testifying to this nightly service. Though supposed to spend his night in bed, he was rarely in his cell.

There was a novice who was at death's door. He was terrified of dying alone. It was past midnight when Brother Martin administered a poultice that was heated.

"How did you know I was in distress?" asked the surprised novice.

Martin caressed the burning brow of the lad, pretending he had not heard the question. "Be not afraid, brother. There is nothing to frighten you. You may feel very ill. But you will not die."

Poor old Father Veresco was in great pain and desperately ill. Too sick to move, he moaned aloud: "If only I had a little hot water to bathe my aching limb." No one could possibly have heard him. Not a soul was astir. But he had barely expressed his wish when Brother Martin entered the room. In his hand was a basin of boiling water.

The strange thing about Martin was his radiant joy. The more patients he had, the happier he seemed. His love of the sick was a vocation within a vocation. His treatment was never haphazard or hurried. He was careful and methodical. He used medical science to the best of his ability. But when medicine failed — then he relied entirely on prayer.

How he had the strength and endurance to accomplish all he did remains a source of mystery. He never wasted a moment. He foresaw needs and planned the day to cope with them to the fullest extent of his abilities. However, the unforseen would happen. Thus he performed his regular duties; then carried out the added burdens as well.

There was, for instance, a horrible epidemic that swept through the city of Lima. This plague caught the people totally unprepared. There was no hospital at the time; no accommodation for tending the thousands stricken unto death. It was not a matter of days, but hours, before they succumbed.

Father Prior sent Brother Martin to relieve and aid where he could in the death-stricken city. When he returned, he ministered unto his own brethren and to sixty novices. No one was left on his feet. Martin worked night and day within his own convent, as well as on the outside.

In his own eyes, Martin was a mere nobody-a creature who neither counted nor had to be considered. He had acquired such utter detachment from material things that they became nonessential. He ate because the rule said he had to eat. Yet what he consumed became a source of total indifference. It mattered not in the least what Brother Refectorian dished out for him; whether the food was stone cold or inadequate for one with a man-sized job to perform.

Very different, indeed, was his concern for man or beast. He made it a personal concern to see that all under his care were properly fed. The sick required special care. Their meals had to be palatable, their diets well-regulated.

The early years in religious life had been exceedingly difficult for Martin. He might have resented the unnecessary suffering and humiliations so mercilessly inflicted on him. He might have succumbed to despair upon recognizing the utter hopelessness and futility of winning over an entire religious establishment. Or he might have become warped and embittered as had his own poor mother.

Instead, he depended — not on creatures — but on God. He expected nothing from his fellow man, looking to them for neither praise nor help. Thus, in turn, he became one of those rare religious: the ethereal, self-effacing type who live for others, never causing the slightest pain or trouble.

Martin had his own cell near the front door. His rough bed consisted of a few boards. Yet he was rarely in that cell. He used it merely for extra prayer or as a place in which to take his daily discipline.

Brother Martin was drawn to the chapter room. There before a lifelike crucifix he spent the night. He found it difficult to detach himself from the gaze of the crucified Christ. When he ended his contemplation, he snatched a few brief hours of sleep at the foot of that cross.

By dawn, he was always awake in time to ring the four o'clock bell. In order to do so, he had to climb the winding tower stairway. He was glad to be the first to greet a new day; to offer this fresh holocaust to his Maker.

When the bell was rung, he hastened to a corner of the garden. There he dug, weeded and transplanted his medicinal herbs. Physically strong, it required a giant constitution to perform the herculean tasks he accomplished. Brother Martin well knew that what he did not attend to himself would, in all probability, be left undone. As a Negro, it was difficult for him to enforce his orders. Though in a position of authority, it had been only by using tact and assuming the most difficult tasks himself that he had accomplished all he did.

Nothing ever escaped his vigilant eye. He was not the type of mystic who hid behind a cloak of asceticism in order to escape reality. Nor did he use his longing for contemplation as an excuse to load the daily burden onto the shoulders of others. Doggedly

Martin made his rounds from one sickbed to another.

Each winter brought its ailments. Martin did not escape. Though consumed by exhausting fevers, Martin never sought respite. There was no time for self. Only when his feet would no longer bear the ailing body did he snatch a few hours of enforced rest. One or two hours was all he allotted himself before resuming his kindly ministrations.

On one occasion, it was the patients who grew alarmed over their feverish and emaciated infirmarian. Father Prior, worried about Martin's physical condition, had ordered him to bed.

"Remember, Brother Martin. When I say bed, I mean it. You are not merely to lie down on your bed of boards. You're to take a mattress and cover it with sheets. You are to go to bed, like everyone else does, properly covered with blankets."

Martin promptly obeyed. He retired to his cell. One of the brethren put in charge of Martin came to see how the patient was doing. Angrily he rushed to Father Prior.

"Brother Martin is impossible. He has flagrantly disobeyed. You gave orders that he was to use sheets and a blanket. The mattress and bedding have been carefully laid on the boards. But I find Brother Martin — lying fully clothed — on top of everything. Will you please insist on obedience? I can do nothing."

Father Prior smiled. "Brother, leave the patient to his own childlike devices. He simply wants to deprive himself of legitimate comforts. We'll permit Martin to carry out his own mode of sanctification. He has obeyed the letter of the law. So, mind your own business and let our humble lay brother practice this added self-denial."

Another time, Father Prior called on Martin. "You are ill, brother. You are to go to bed at once. On one previous occasion, I closed my eyes to your unique method of self-abnegation. But today you need utter relaxation. So do as I bid you. Go to bed like everyone else does. You are at others' beck and call night and day, year in and year out. Take off your habit and give yourself a good rest."

Brother Martin, who could never be induced to sleep between

sheets, pleaded humbly: "In my own home, I had neither bread, wine, sheets nor a pillow. Here in this convent, where I have come to dedicate my life to God, I have all these luxuries. You bid me to lie down and rest on a comfortable bed. But what right has a poor man like me to such luxuries?"

Father Prior shook his head. "Brother, you are a hopeless renegade. Go your way, then. God seems to bless your methods. They must be meant for you."

Martin's love for poverty was just as extraordinary. It was remarkable how he managed to get along without ever asking anything for himself. His clothing was always of the poorest quality — old and worn. He disliked slovenliness. He could not tolerate rags.

Handy with a needle, he patched his habit like a tailor. Jokingly he claimed that the older, the more patched his habit became, the surer he was of being in style. When pressed to accept a new habit, he seemed hurt.

"Why, I have two perfectly good habits. Are they not sufficient? When the one is soiled, I wash it. What in heaven's name would I do with a third one?"

Through his habits and scapular might be patched and even darned beyond recognition, so that none of the original material was to be found, his clothes were always spotless. His habit was his uniform—worn in the service of God. As such, he kept it with the same pride as that of a soldier maintaining his uniform for dress parade.

Shoes always seemed to Martin to be superfluous. He still had an innate repugnance to wearing new ones. When a new pair was forced on him, he smilingly accepted. Then, slyly, he would lend them to some beggar on the condition that when they were old and shabby, he would not discard them. Martin wanted them back again.

When reprimanded for his lack of obedience, Martin replied: "Perhaps I am wrong. But when wearing new shoes, I have to be doubly careful of them. They have to be shined and I must always think of protecting them from abuse. But when wearing the old ones, I never have to think of my feet. Besides, if I lost a pair of new shoes, I'd be commmitting a very grave fault. However, if I should misplace these, the loss would be small. The fault, therefore, would not be as serious."

Though Brother Martin always selected for himself the worst in clothing, he was deeply concerned about the requirements of the brethren. There happened to occur a period of great want during which the convent had no money. The Dominicans were too poor to buy the expensive white wool material. The result was that all the community went about in sadly-patched habits. Martin could not bear the thought of priests looking so shabby and threadbare.

In Lima some of the most noted merchants had been former patients of his. Brother Martin made the rounds of the wholesale houses. The fabric merchants were apprised of the situation. A few days thereafter, the tailors within Holy Rosary Convent were busily cutting out brand-new habits. The merchants had rallied to Martin's plea. They had gladly sent sufficient material to clothe the entire community.

Martin liked to see the religious exert special care in regard to their personal appearance. He felt this was appropriate due to their station in life. Were they not representatives of Christ? As such, nothing careless or slovenly was seemly.

One day, while on an errand with an old priest, they passed a young secular priest who had been roundly criticized by many of the clergy. They said he was too finicky, too meticulous about his clothes. Turning to Martin, his elderly companion remarked:

"What do you say about a man in orders who goes about as vainly as does Father Martinau?"

Martin looked sad. "We are not fit judges. I am sure he does this out of respect for the people with whom he associates. Souls have to be drawn to God by outward appearances and signs. Thus he shows his good sense. Can't you see for yourself how this priest—by his elegance of manner, his pleasing ways, his great charity—brings people to him instead of repulsing them?

"You, dear father, are very holy. Yet you have just the contrary effect on people. They are afraid of your austerity. Your ragged habit repulses them. Just look at your slovenly shoes. They are miles too big. No. . . . you cannot condemn this young priest. Were I a sinner looking for a confessor — in all truth, dear father, I'd run away from you. You'd frighten me. This young man would attract me."

Once again, the depression that had engulfed Lima and all of South America knocked at the convent doors. Father Prior was exhausted from begging tours. He had even gone so far as to ask banking firms to lend him a sizeable sum. Martin knew that, as a doctor, he was in great demand. He also knew that if he gave his services to the town, it would gladly pay a handsome sum. He knocked at Father Prior's door. He explained that, since financial aid was so slow in coming, why not sell his services?

"After all, I am nothing better than a slave. I am insignificant. Others are in need. Since I belong to the convent, you are perfectly free to treat me in the same manner as you would handle any of the other slaves on the property. I'm entirely at your disposal. I'll gladly do whatever I can to be of use."

Father Prior was deeply moved. The more he saw of Martin, the more he marveled. Each time he thought he had reached a fuller understanding of the lay brother, invariably he was to learn there was still another side yet more astounding.

He dismissed Brother Martin, thanking him but assuring him that as long as Holy Rosary Convent stood, he would be amongst its members as a free man.

11
Brother Rat And
Bedtime Stories

Brother Martin loved nature passionately. On seeing a flower, he would be transported with joy. In his medicinal garden there was a special corner reserved for ornamental flowers. His roses were the most beautiful in all Lima.

With pride, he placed his prize roses at the Shrine of the Madonna. No matter how busy during the day, he usually managed to slip through his garden. On returning, he would carry a bright nosegay which he left as a tribute of love. For, to him — the Blessed Virgin was a real mother. In fact, the only mother he had ever known. His devotion to her was alive and ardent.

Brother Martin always considered flowers and animals to be God's handiwork. They were merely reflections of the Maker's beauty. The whole world mirrored God.

From his earliest childhood, Martin had shown particular affection and understanding for animals. They, in turn, came to Martin at all times; but especially when in trouble. It was a matter of constant occurrence for the doctor, while making his rounds, to pick up stray animals. As a child, had he not been punished — in season and out of season — for bringing home birds and baby animals that he had rescued?

This habit was to persist throughout Martin's life, resulting in a collection of tales. The children of Lima; then, later — of all South America — loved to hear about Brother Martin. He and his animals became bedtime stories that put them to sleep.

One of his very special pets was a brilliantly plumaged rooster. During a barnyard fight, the young cock had been badly hurt. As Martin was about to enter the home of a client, he noticed an inanimate mass of feathers. He carried it indoors, reviving it with water. The bleeding cock had a broken leg. Doctor de Porrez bound it up in a splint, giving orders that it was to be segregated for a few days and cared for.

From then on, whenever Martin went through that particular section of town, a row of curious hens cackled their greeting. Then out would march the proud, crowing rooster — as if to say a personal how-do-you-do. Appointing himself bodyguard, he would then escort the doctor for several blocks. In fact — had he not been sent home, the rooster would have followed Martin about like a dog.

With two companions, Brother Martin had been sent by Father Prior to supervise the picking of cotton on a distant estate owned by the convent. Brother Martin was struck by the grace, strength and swift flight of an eagle that he was watching. From a distance, a farmer was also peering at the eagle. But instead of admiration, hatred was written on his face. The bird of prey had killed his chickens and wounded his lambs. Taking aim with his shotgun, he fired — the wounded eagle falling to the ground like a rock.

Brother Martin started toward it, determined to go to its rescue. He went no further because his companions held him back. The enormous bird was flapping its huge wings — ready to tear to pieces anyone who approached.

Brother Martin spoke softly, melodiously: "Come now, Brother Eagle. Stay where you are. Your wings won't carry you. So stop your flapping. I won't hurt you — King of Birds. I won't harm you if you'll only let me see what you're suffering from."

The eagle blinked its wild eyes and cocked its head; then lay motionless. Each time Brother Martin got close enough to touch the bird, his companions pleaded: "Don't go nearer. You'll be torn from head to foot by that dangerous beak and those fierce talons. Let it die. No one will ever miss it."

Brother Martin lifted the huge bird onto the pommel of his saddle. People along the road stopped to stare at the strange sight: Brother Martin in his blood-stained white habit and a half-dead eagle.

At the monastery, everyone fled when Martin carried the eagle to his own cell. There he nursed the bird. After a while, it became quite tame — hopping about the room and waiting for Martin to come and feed it. The friars were as deathly afraid of the eagle as if it had been the plague.

Early one morning, after Brother Martin had rung the rising bell, he returned to his cell. He carried the heavy bird to the garden. By now, it readily perched on his shoulder. After bidding his newly-made friend farewell, he told it to fly to freedom. The eagle stretched its wings, flapped them powerfully; then — heading towards the sun — flew away.

Every morning after that, while Martin worked in his garden, he would hear a repetition of the flapping and whir of wings. The eagle had found a home in nearby woods. No sooner did Martin appear each dawn than the eagle would come to keep him company. Sometimes he would perch on the wall. More often he would follow Martin — who, while digging — often unearthed worms. To these the eagle helped himself.

From then on, Martin was never disturbed by any stray guests. Word had been passed that the eagle followed Martin everywhere he went in his garden. No one cared to risk an encounter with the powerful predator.

There was an enormous black dog that lived near the monastery. Every time any members of the community left the convent gate, they were bound to encounter the ferocious beast. People had complained bitterly. By both its barking and biting, the dog had proved to be a menace as well as a nuisance.

Brother Martin was the only one whom "Nero" respected. He used to shake his finger at the animal.

"You naughty dog. . . what do you mean by terrifying all passersby? Some day you'll get into trouble. You'll meet another dog fiercer and stronger than you are. Why don't you mind your own business, instead of being jealous when any man or beast passes your home?"

Then "Nero" would slink away. But, apparently, he soon forgot his sermon. For, in a short while, he was back — pursuing both dogs and humans.

On a certain morning, Brother Martin was in a great hurry. There was an urgent errand he had to attend to in town. As he hastily left the convent, he was accosted by "Nero." This time — not the wild, aggressive "Nero" that barked and bellowed; but a whimpering dog covered with blood from deep wounds. Pitifully "Nero" looked at Martin, as if to say: "Look at what has happened to me. Please help me."

Martin shook his head, gently petting the suffering animal. "Well. . . 'Nero.' You're an absolute disgrace. Did I not warn you that no good would come of your nasty temper? You've got what you deserve. Now that you're in a mess — you expect me to sew you up.

"Well. . . I'll do it — but on one condition only. Remember you're never to fight again. It just is not nice. Everyone hates you and you're really a likeable animal. Come along. . . we'll go back to the house." The dog followed Brother Martin meekly as a lamb.

In his cell, Brother Martin washed and dressed the wounds. He cared for the dog till its sores were healed. Everyone teased the infirmarian, wondering what he would next bring to his cell. Some began to grumble. It was contrary to monastic spirit for a convent to be turned into a zoo.

But "Nero" did not bother anyone. He never barked or growled. He stayed obediently where Brother Martin put him.

When the time came for "Nero" to be sent home, Brother Martin spoke sharply. The dog slunk to the ground — his tail between his legs. He could not have been more dejected had Brother Martin whipped him.

"Now — go home, 'Nero.' But, remember. No more nonsense. Don't you ever again be a naughty dog. You've had more than enough suffering to last for quite a while."

Then, when Brother Martin had petted "Nero" — the dog rose, licked his hand and raised its paw to bid farewell. Wagging its tail, it ran home briskly. Never again was "Nero" a bad-tempered animal. Brother Martin had taught him his manners.

Father Procurator, who had charge of the convent's finances, had a dog of his own. For a period of eighteen years, "Fidelis" had never left his master. He had been a devoted companion and an excellent pet. Father Procurator had taken the dog's fidelity for granted.

When "Fidelis" grew a bit lame with old age and his coat turned an ugly color and his appearance somewhat scraggly and moth-eaten, Father Procurator decided to dispose of "Fidelis." He sent for one of the convent slaves who was very fond of "Fidelis."

"Here. . . take this *stiletto*," he said. "And take 'Fidelis' to the meadow at the other end of the convent. You're not to speak of this to anyone. We can't go on, having a good-for-nothing animal hanging about the place."

Though the poor Indian pleaded to be permitted to keep "Fidelis," Father Procurator was adamant. He had given his orders. The slave had to obey.

Though grieved, the heartbroken slave led "Fidelis" to his doom. On reaching the deserted medow, he used the *stiletto*. He had made a stab at the dog, but lacked the heart to finish his dirty work. As the dog whimpered in pain, the slave fled in horror.

Just as this was taking place, Brother Martin was returning to the convent. He had taken a shortcut, which ran across the deserted meadow. He had heard the cries of a dog in anguish, had seen the Indian flee. Suspecting that poor "Fidelis" might be the victim, he searched till he found the tortured animal — still alive.

Brother Martin tenderly carried "Fidelis" back to the convent in his arms. He stitched up the gaping wound as best he could; then nursed the dog back to health. He had said nothing of this to anyone.

Meanwhile, Father Procurator had told everyone that poor, faithful, old "Fidelis" had died a natural death. Thus it was to his utter amazement and consternation that, one day, he saw Brother Martin walking down the corridor with a dog that very much resembled his former "Fidelis" — except that this animal walked briskly and was carefully groomed.

As they passed, he asked dumbfounded: "Brother, where did you get that dog?"

"Fidelis" cowed at Martin's feet — afraid to meet the eyes of his former master.

"That's my dog," said Father Procurator to the Father Provincial.

"Why, your dog died a natural death," reminded Father Provincial. "So how could you possibly claim this is your dog?"

Then the provincial congratulated Brother Martin. "My. . . what a nice-looking dog you have there. He seems to be very devoted to you."

Brother Martin smiled. He continued stroking the dog's head. "Don't be afraid, 'Fidelis.' He can do you no more harm. But just remember to keep away from Father Procurator in the future. After eighteen years of faithful service, he ordered you to be cruelly killed. Though you were his best friend and his most faithful companion — that's how he rewarded your fidelity. But fear nothing. I will personally care for you always. He's unworthy to have so noble a dog."

Needless to say, Father Procurator hastily retraced his steps with a very red face. Father Provincial stroked the old dog's head and remarked:

"You're lucky, 'Fidelis' — to have found so kind a friend and benefactor at the end of your life."

From then on, whenever "Fidelis" saw his former master, he turned and fled — much to the amusement of the rest of the community and to Father Procurator's acute embarrassment.

One day, while crossing the slums of Lima, Martin was astonished by a loud commotion. That section of town was usually drab and silent, sullenly silent. Yet, today, a noisy crowd had gathered — laughing loudly and coarsely.

Martin stopped at the fringe of the crowd to witness a very poor Indian trying to rescue his donkey. Martin elbowed his way to the front of the crowd, which consisted mostly of Spanish with a sprinkling of Negroes. The little gray donkey had passed too close to a dangerous gully. It had been raining and the clay soil had given way. Weighed down by its heavy load of faggots, the animal was floundering helplessly in the quagmire.

The Indian called, he yelled. Each time the animal heard his master's voice, he struggled wildly to climb the perpendicular wall. But each time, instead of freeing himself, he only became more hopelessly entangled in the mud and rocks.

The frantic Indian had done everything within his power. Now he begged the onlookers to lend a helping hand. But they only roared the louder, rocking with laughter. They thought it most amusing to watch the little donkey sink deeper and deeper into the mire. Besides, why should they help an Indian?

Brother Martin turned to the Indian. "Can't someone get down there and remove the wood from the back of the donkey? It might then have a chance to regain its footing."

With tears in his eyes, the Indian shook his head. "For the past hour, I have tried to get help. My poor beast is now exhausted. He no longer has any strength left. What am I to do? I dare not go home without my faithful donkey that has served me so well.

"He carts my vegetables to market and brings bales of cotton and sugarcane to town when in season. Today we had gone for wood, which I hoped to store against the winter. Tomorrow we were to bring down a supply of potatoes from the mountains. Now I'll have to cart the wood, the sugar, the cotton and the potatoes on my own back.

"I'm too poor to afford the price of a new donkey. Besides, no man could have had a more faithful friend than this. Yet not a soul will now help me save him."

Martin was annoyed by the curelty of these callous people. "Do not lose heart," he encouraged, leaning over the pit. "I will see what I can do."

"You mean well, kind friend," said the Indian. "But it's too late. In a few more minutes, my donkey will perish in the quicksand. You, alone, can do nothing. It would require the help of at least four or five strong men."

Martin made a large Sign of the Cross over the pit. Then, in a loud voice, called:

"Come, creature of God. In the name of the Creator Who made you — I command you to come forth."

To the noisy ruffians, this was even more hilarious than the donkey's pitiful plight. They hooted in derision. They scoffed at the

Negro lay brother, at the man with the white habit and the very black face.

Then there was silence. . . a shocked and appalling silence. The little donkey had struggled once more. Its load of faggots — heavy and sodden from the muddy soaking — balanced precariously to the right and to the left. Then, miraculously, the plucky beast regained its footing. And, before the eyes of the hushed assemblage, it walked up the side of the steep incline — to stand trembling before its incredulous and overjoyed master.

When the Indian turned to thank Brother Martin, he found he had vanished. The crowd slunk away — shamefaced by its cowardice.

On another day, Brother Martin had been summoned to the deathbed of a former patient. The woman was poor and old. Her son had come to the convent, pleading that Martin do something to save his mother.

As the two were crossing the beautiful square in front of the Cathedral, they heard terrified screams. They saw a huge crowd of men and women rushing to seek shelter within the walls of the Cathedral. Some fifteen or twenty panicky children were trying to follow their elders. But they were too slow to catch up with them.

As Martin ran forward to help the struggling children, he saw they were fleeing from a wild bull. There was not a moment to lose. The charging animal was bearing down on several of the smaller tots. It would be but a matter of seconds before he trampled them to death in his fury.

Brother Martin had but one thought. At all costs —he must stop the bull before he reached the children. Throwing his habit over his arm, he bounded forward as if in a racing contest. As he confronted the raging beast, he stopped and held up his hand.

"Brother Bull. . . pacify yourself. Contain your ferocious temper. You have no right to harm any of God's creatures."

The wild bull came to a full stop. Snorting and pawing the ground with rage, the beast lowered his great head for the charge. The onlookers, safe upon the Cathedral steps, shrieked with fear. They warned Martin that he would be gored unmercifully. But Martin did not move. The two long, sharp horns seemed to encircle the lay brother. They must have been fully two feet long. As the horns reached the ground, Brother Martin raised his hand and caressed the great head of the bull.

"Come. . ." he said, stepping to one side and seizing an ear, which he then used like a halter. "I must bring you back to your master. In the future, don't run through the heart of the city. If you need exercise —wait till youg get in God's beautiful fields and meadows."

Brother Martin had a very special liking for mice and rats. He felt they were really the most abused of all God's creatures. People either shunned them or killed them mercilessly. He made pets of rats and mice. He taught the convent cats to make friends with these rodents. In Martin's cell, cats, mice and rats daily ate out of the same dish.

Most of the friars felt very differently about the matter. They were disgusted by Martin's perverse taste. For a long time, Brother Martin did all he could to defend his pets. Then one of the friars complained that rats and mice were always gnawing holes in his stockings. Brother Martin assured him that if he were less untidy and hung up his clothes, instead of throwing them on the floor, he would not be sorely tempting the hungry rodents.

But rats being rats and mice being mice, their numbers rapidly swelled and multiplied. At first, Brother Martin became somewhat dismayed, then alarmed. The appetite of his ever-increasing pets had assumed enormous proportions. They no longer confined themselves to nibbling cheese in the larder or corn in the corn bin. They overran the convent. They implanted their sharp teeth and satisfied their keen appetites in the most outlandish and unbecoming manner.

This insatiable appetite of theirs was the cause of their undoing. Father Prior felt he had been patient long enough. He and the friars were up in arms. Something would have to be done; for even the privacy of Father Prior's cell had finally been invaded. His Sunday scapular, which he had left carefully folded the evening before, was now riddled with holes.

The rats and mice no longer had any respect for the studious friars. They disturbed their well-earned rest at night by scrambling across their beds. By day, they played hide-and-seek, scurrying from desk to desk. They tasted the gold leaf, scampered through paint and left the mark of their paws on priceless parchments.

The community bell convoked the friars to the chapter room for an extraordinary meeting. Father Prior informed them that, on the morrow, the day would be spent in exterminating rats. Traps would be set. Poison would be used. Every known method would be employed to rid the convent once and for all of the pesky rodents.

Each of the friars left the chapter room with his hands tucked beneath his scapular, his head bent low in contemplation. Alone in his thoughts and purpose, Brother Martin was not contemplating; nor was he conversing with God. Brother Martin was enduring a conflict. He was weighing in the balance of his mind whether he should blindly obey the order and do as the others; or could he, in time, devise some means of saving his little friends.

On reaching his cell, he had an inspiration. He carefully closed the door. Then he whistled the low, shrill whistle he always used to summon his favorite rat. Almost immediately — out of a hole to the right of his room — peered an inquisitive head. The rat emerged and began to clean his long, imposing whiskers.

"Brother Rat. . . Brother Rat!" exclaimed Martin. "Waste no time in idle play. I have something of importance to tell you."

The rat hurried to the foot of the simple wooden table. He leapt to the table and sat on Brother Martin's hand.

"Brother Rat, what's happened to the appetite of your family? They are all your children. I have warned you to admonish them and told you they must be more cautious.

"I know, dear Brother Rat, God seems to have given you all tremendous appetites. But you might have confined and restricted your tastes. Instead, you've overstepped your bounds. You've taken advantage of my patience. I do not rule here. I am merely a servant of the servants of God. You'll have to stop feasting on clothing and linens and bedding and sacred vestments. Your appetite has no bounds.

"Little Brother, you're in exceedingly grave danger. Tomorrow, the prior had told us, every one of you is to be exterminated. You are all to be killed. So go immediately and warn your family of this unhappy verdict. They must abandon the convent at once."

The poor old rat trembled with fear. His beady eyes stared at Brother Martin, as if to ask: "What must we do? We are at your mercy."

Brother Martin nodded. "There is one alternative. Collect your children and grandchildren and greatgrandchildren. Let them follow you to the abandoned barn at the far end of the garden. No one has used it for years. You'll be safe there. I will see to it that you get food, so you won't starve.

"Remember, though, that not one of you is ever to show his head inside the convent again. If any of you should disobey me, I'll wash my hands of the consequences. Now hurry. . . hurry. Be off, Brother Rat, and be quick about your mission."

Brother Martin had patients to tend in the infirmary. By the time he had climbed the stairs, the peaceful convent had turned into a madhouse. Its customary silence was broken by curses and yells. Doors slammed, furniture crashed, dishes smashed to the ground. Bedlam and pandemonium reigned.

It sounded as if the place had become the abode of demons; not of saintly men who had consecrated their lives to the preaching of the gospels and the study of church history. Sedate priests sought refuge on windowsills, on tables, on beds. They were convinced that the devil in person had come to tempt and scare them. Rats and mice had startled them.

A large percentage of the community had been assembled for the noonday meal in the refectory. The Brother Lector had found his reading impaired when a monstrous rat perched itself unexpectedly on top of the very book from which he was reading. It was as if the brute were giving orders. It turned its head to the right and then to the left.

Brother Lector ceased reading — so great was his fright. Father Prior rang the bell, admonishing him to continue.

Then — from the right and from the left — rats and mice

suddenly tore across the long room. The marble floor was not wide enough to hold the stream of densely-packed rodents. So they raced down the long refectory tables, splashing in and out of the plates, upsetting glasses and getting lost in platters.

In the kitchen, there was the same commotion. From behind copper pots and pans darted rats and mice. From the sugar bin, the corncrib, the dairy and the meat house — they poured.

Father Prior ordered the meal to be interrupted. Grace was said. The much-disgusted brethren felt this surely must be some sort of visitation by way of punishment for their premeditated plan to exterminate the rats.

As they reached the stairs, they halted speechless. There were rats. . . more rats. An ever-increasing stream of rats — bounding down the corridor! There were fat rats and lean ones. There were big rats and small mice. There were rats of every breed and every color. Finally, there came scurrying fluffy, little soft-gray balls. Even the baby mice had joined in the melee.

Father Prior instantly suspected that Brother Martin had had a hand in this extraordinary sortie. He found him, as he had been sure he would, in the infirmary.

"What does this mean?" demanded the prior indignantly.

Brother Martin looked apologetic. "Father Prior, I promise you that never again will you or the friars be troubled by these little creatures. It was most unfortunate that they discovered our white wool habits made soft, downy nests for their young; that the gold brocaded vestments tasted sweeter than cheese or corn; or that they acquired a liking for expensive laces and upholstery.

"You have been very patient with me and my pets. But they'll not bother you again. They have sought refuge in the empty barn at the other end of the garden. From this window, you can see them — this very moment — heading toward their new abode."

Father Prior smiled to himself. Would Brother Martin never grow up? Would he always continue taking the side of the neglected, the persecuted and the forsaken? But as he gazed from the window, he saw that Martin had spoken the truth. The very rats and mice that had disrupted luncheon were now vanishing in unison into the recesses of the abandoned barn.

"I hope, Brother Martin, you will keep the rats and mice in control in the future. Never again are they to upset any household such as they have mine."

Brother Martin promised. From that time on, whenever rats or mice troubled any of the citizens of Lima to any great extent, Brother Martin would always be sent for. On such occasions, he brought along with him a new broom. Then he would place this broom behind the kitchen door, after having first invoked a special prayer. As long as the broom remained in place, no mouse or rat ever crossed the threshold of that home.

Years later — even centuries after Brother Martin's death — people in Latin America still kept little wisps from the original brooms distributed by Brother Martin to scare off rats and mice.

In Lima there was a man who had once been extremely wealthy. Then came the depression. No matter how hard Senor Rodriguez tried to save his estate, everything he had trickled away like water. He lost his money and was reduced to penury. He went from door to door trying to find work. Nowhere could he gain employment.

At last, very early one morning, he came to the convent. He hoped no one would see him. Sênor Rodriguez was ashamed of his poverty, ashamed of the fact that he had come begging to Brother Martin.

Martin welcomed him like a long-lost friend and took him to his cell. There, with tears in his eyes, Senor Rodriguez explained that he was destitute. His tale of woe was great. At home — now merely a poor adobe hovel — lay his dying wife. His eight children were starving. The little ones had had nothing to eat for several days.

Brother Martin was distressed. "How unfortunate that you have come to me at such a moment. Personally, I have not a single thing I can offer to alleviate your need.

"Look about my cell. You can see for yourself how the whitewashed walls have been stripped of every ornament. Even the crucifix which I prized has gone. What little remains — such as the bench, table and the wooden boards, comprising my bed —

Frightened and fully expecting to be accused of theft, Señor Rodriguez explained: "It was given me by Brother Martin at the convent. He told me to pawn it here."

"Good. . . good," smiled the pawnbroker, entirely satisfied. "Anything that comes from Brother Martin is worth its weight in gold. Never before have I seen anything to equal this ruby. Señor, you're in luck. I can dispose of it quickly for ready cash."

"But this jewel is not for sale. I merely wish to pawn it."

"My good man — are you crazy? You're poor. What can you want with such a valuable jewel?" Then he pulled out a purse filled with gold. He began to count the coins, tossing them onto the counter.

"Stop. . . stop," said Señor Rodriguez. "I told you this is not for sale. No offer on your part will tempt me to break my word to Brother Martin."

The pawnbroker sneered. "You fool. As if that Negro could know the value of this jewel! Tell him you have lost it. Tell him you have sold it. Or replace it with a substitute. There are a thousand and one ways you can get around your promise."

"I'm sorry, Sir. But unless you do as I request, I'll be obliged to go elsewhere."

Because of his firmness, Señor Rodriguez secured the money he needed. He minutely carried out Brother Martin's instructions.

A few months later, a well-dressed man returned to the pawnshop. He produced his ticket and re-claimed his ruby.

"I refuse to part with this jewel," said the pawnbroker with lustful eyes.

"No bickering on your part will change my mind. I'm on my way now to the convent to return my indebtedness."

"You fool!" shouted the broker. "Don't you know enough to take advantage of a good thing when you hold it in your hand?"

Señor Rodriguez paid no attention. As soon as he replaced the sparkling jewel in its box, he returned to the convent. There he met Brother Martin. Together they went to the little whitewashed cell.

"How can I ever express to you my gratitude for all you have done for me? For entrusting me with so priceless a treasure?"

Brother Martin smiled as he held out his hand. "Yes, Sēnor. You are right. All of God's handiwork is priceless. It can never be duplicated."

Though Brother Martin had not yet opened the box to examine the contents, he bent towards the floor. With one hand — he now opened the lid. And the ruby rolled to the ground.

Sēnor Rodriguez remembered what the pawnbroker had said. How could a simple monk know the value of that dazzling jewel?

"Brother Martin. . . I beg of you to be careful. You'll injure the ruby. It will get scratched and marred. Did you know it is worth a fortune?"

Brother Martin may or may not have heard Sēnor Rodriguez. In any event, he made no comment. Instead, he was now gazing intently at the ruby — which had suddenly begun to move. It had acquired legs. It walked across the room to a spider web. Having climbed to the center of its web, it started spinning new strands.

Sēnor Rodriguez fell on his knees. "What's this?" he cried. "My priceless ruby is a simple red spider?"

"Yes," smiled Brother Martin. "As I said before — God is good. . . very good. And His handiwork is priceless."

12
Father Of The Poor

Once Brother Martin found himself in an embarrassing position. He had been approached by former wealthy clients presently reduced to penury. They had sold their clothes to feed their children. Now they had come, seeking clothing and help. Brother Martin was forced to tell them he had nothing on hand. As usual, he had given away his last *centavo.*

Then he remembered he was custodian of his sister's dowry. A rich friend had heard of Juana's poverty. Feeling sorry for Martin's sister and wishing her to have the happiness of wedded

difficulties, your union must and will succeed. But only if both of you meet each other halfway."

Martin had taken both completely by surprise. They had no idea he had heard of their trials and difficulties. Seeing that they were ashamed, Martin changed the conversation.

"Come. . . let's have a party. I've brought food enough for all the neighbors. Invite them so we may all celebrate."

Martin knew there was nothing so conducive to good humor as a jovial party. When the guests had assembled, he blessed the meal. Everyone was astonished by the unexpected turn of events. The storm had passed. The tenseness had disappeared.

Later that evening, when Juana wished to thank her brother for what he had done, she went to his room — but found he had gone.

From then on, neither Juana nor her husband was ever again to waste time in quarrels. Their home became a model of happiness. The entire neighborhood, which before had been so occupied in spreading nasty gossip, was now just as loud in singing their praise.

Soon the news spread. Brother Martin was often called upon thereafter to settle marital problems. Disputes were brought to him. Husbands and wives sought his advice. Over and over again, he salvaged homes that were about to be shipwrecked. He rescued parents and children by his sympathetic understanding of their personal problems.

Martin began to be known as "Lima's Angel of Peace." For, the Spaniards and the mulattos had fiery tempers and sharp tongues. Unfortunately, they were often too proud to apologize or retract their hastily spoken words. A visit with Brother Martin worked wonders.

Martin's charity was not confined to the grown-ups. He loved children—especially the poor children, who usually were in hot water. These he constantly defended and often protected.

If a poor student needed tutoring, it was at Martin's door that he knocked. If a group of boys needed money badly — they, too, found his cell. To these he entrusted his herb garden; or would provide special errands to run for which he no longer had the time. These services were paid out of donations given him by wealthy Spanish potentates.

On one occasion, he gave an important letter to one of these boys. The lad carefully unsealed the letter, opening it and reading its contents. The next day, Martin roundly reprimanded him for his lack of honesty. The astonished culprit never knew how Martin found out because he had made a point of resealing the envelope so his act could not be detected.

On another occasion, a group of very hungry boys pleaded for a meal. Brother Martin had been arranging a basket of fruit for one of his sick patients. He left it sitting on the table of his cell while he rushed to the kitchen to see what else he could round up.

While he was absent, the boys ate the fruit. Then one of their number sneaked open the table drawer. On seeing a gold piece, he slyly slipped it into his shoe, knowing that no one would detect it there.

When Brother Martin returned with a steaming bowl of stew, he remarked: "Boys. . . I'm certainly glad you enjoyed the fruit — though it really was meant for a very poor, sick, old priest. This I will gladly pardon. But the money you have taken must be returned. It is not mine. It was given to me for a very specific purpose."

The boys were aghast. "What money? Where? None of us has seen any. What do you take us for. . . thieves?"

Brother Martin replied very quietly: "I am sorry, boys. But the money I had in this table drawer is gone. One of you has taken it."

Again the boys were annoyed, even angry. One of them asked: "How can you accuse us of stealing money from a drawer when you have not even looked to see it it is there? Are you doubting our honesty?"

"One of your group has taken the money. John. . . you are the wrongdoer. Kindly return what is not yours."

John blushed but flatly denied the theft. His companions defended him.

Brother Martin waited till the tumult died down. Then he ordered: "John — take off your right shoe. Otherwise, I'll have to

one of his closest friends. The Archbishop of Mexico revered him like a saint. He never came to town that he did not insist that Brother Martin join him at his table for a good, substantial meal. Poor Brother Martin was invariably confused when this prelate would give him the place of honor, seating him above all the Spanish dignitaries.

Whenever a priest required a favor, it was Martin whom he first approached. Somehow, Brother Martin had been endowed with the tact and ability of a statesman. He knew how to plead and how to solve difficulties. Thus he became the intermediary for everyone in town. His duties were unending and assumed tremendous proportions.

Even within the convent, the friction once caused by racial prejudice had vanished. Instead — he was esteemed and revered by the brethren, who appreciated his charity and his zeal.

Martin was a firm believer in avoiding the devil. He felt that Satan was all-powerful and had best be shunned. Late one evening, Martin was loaded down with an armful of medicine bottles and a burning brazier. One of his patients was very ill. He had gone to the kitchen to heat some ointment and prepare a poultice. As he rounded the dangerous corner of the narrow infirmary stairs, he came to face with a horrible creature. As Martin tried to advance, he was prevented from going any further.

Displaying his usual common sense, Martin stopped in his tracks. He bent down and set his medicines on the stairs. Then, taking a burning coal from the glowing brazier — he traced a huge Sign of the Cross on the wall.

"What are you doing?" asked the devil.

Martin loosened his broad leather belt and lashed at the devil, saying: "Begone, Satan. Let me look after my own interests."

Then there followed such a wild howl, emitting from that part of the building, that the brethren jumped from their beds to see what had happened.

The next day Brother Martin erected a wooden cross at the exact spot where he had had the encounter the night before. Every night from then on, he lighted a vigil light. Never again was Satan to disturb Martin on that passageway.

When Doctor de Porrez first entered the Convent of the Holy Rosary, his clients felt that he would soon be back in their midst; or else would be permitted to serve them from the convent. Unfortunately, his superiors were of a very different opinion. Brother Martin had sought to retire from the world and did not intend to return to it. He was far too useful within the convent walls.

Brother Martin's former clients began to miss him. But, even more, they wanted and needed him. From time to time, a delegation of his former friends would approach Father Provincial, pleading that he release their much-needed doctor to them. It had been a serious mistake for Martin to abandon his profession. The town was overrun with quack physicians — unscrupulous doctors who charged exorbitant fees but did nothing to cure ailing bodies.

Father Provincial merely turned a deaf ear to all the petitions. Brother Martin was in the convent and there he would remain.

Exasperated that their demands went unheeded; that there were so few reliable doctors; that charlatans were bleeding the poor and were killing — instead of curing — the townsfolk decided to take things into their own hands.

They stormed the convent, shouting morning, noon and even during the night: "Give us back our Martin. He is our doctor. He belongs to the poor and to our people. We need him to cure the sick and to pray over the dying. We want him to bury our dead. . . to feed our starving. No one else will do. We must have our Brother Martin."

The populace finally succeeded in having its way. Father Provincial consented on one condition. Brother Martin could devote his free time to them.

Fortunately — or, perhaps, unfortunately — Father Provincial had no notion, whatsoever, of the size of Brother Martin's former practice. No sooner was permission granted than a steady stream of patients flocked to see Brother Martin.

There was only one hospital in town. It was poor and inadequate.

single slice of bread reserved for the meals of slaves.

Then he rushed back to his diagnoses. Before making any examination, he always waited a second or two, collecting his thoughts and praying that God might direct him.

Martin had the gift of healing to a remarkable degree. One of the priests in Lima had suffered a bad hemorrhage. Terrified at the thought of dying, he did not wait till Brother Martin came to see him. He had himself carried to the convent. As he entered the room, Brother Martin reproached him for his lack of faith.

"Dear father. . . why this haste? There is no need for my diagnosing of your ailment. There is holy water in the fount at the door of my cell. Sprinkle yourself with this sacramental. God will take care of you."

The priest did as he had been told. From then on, he never again had the slightest trouble.

Brother Porter found it exceedingly difficult to fathom Brother Martin. He could readily understand how it was that the poor flocked to him for help. But why did the rich also stand for hours, patiently awaiting their turn?

Of course, Brother Martin never showed any preferences. But had he done so, it would have been for the poor. When the wealthy came, they were treated exactly as if they had been in the lower social and economic brackets. To both rich and poor, alike, he gave the selfsame devoted service.

By interesting the wealthy in the fate of their less-fortunate brethren, Brother Martin hoped he might be able to induce them to give financial aid to the destitute. This was the sole reason why he accommodated them.

Once again, as they had in the past, everyone was talking about the wonderful cures wrought by Brother Martin.

One of the outstanding Spaniards in Lima was Don Juan de Figueroa. As a statesman, it was imperative that he give speeches throughout Latin America. Yet he had a throat ailment which confined him to bed. He sent one of his slaves to bring Brother Martin to him. The doctor examined the patient and gave him a bottle of medicine to take during the course of the morning.

After Martin had left, Don Juan de Figueroa swallowed a spoonful as directed. He was astonished to find that the medication was pure water. He had consulted specialists, but none of them had brought him any relief. Yet the simple potion of drinking water prescribed by Brother Martin effected a complete cure.

One of the servants of the household, upon learning of the remarkable cure, asked permission to try some of the remedy. He was suffering from a horrible skin disease. He, too, was cured as quickly as the master had been.

Juana rushed to her brother. Her favorite slave had fractured his skull. Juana knew there was little hope for his recovery, but the slave had called for Martin. Would he come? Brother Martin reached the house in time to save still another life.

Lady Elizabeth Ortiz de Torrez had gone to Spain to find a doctor who would cure her. For years she had suffered from an internal malady for which there was no known remedy.

Brother Martin was called to her bedside. Instead of ordering a lot of medication, he gave her a nice red apple. Lady de Torrez stared at him in astonishment.

"Eat this slowly. . ." was all that Martin said.

By the time she had finished munching her red apple, Brother Martin was already tending to another patient. Lady de Torrez was cured. She, who had not been able to get up and walk for years, now went in person to thank him for his help.

On another occasion, a poor beggar was cured of a frightful ulcer. All that Brother Martin had done was to make the Sign of the Cross.

Brother Martin had a difficult mission to accomplish. He had chosen as traveling companion one Juan Vasquez. But on the day of their departure, Juan could not move. His feet were unrecognizable, being so badly swollen with rheumatism. Brother Martin examined them; then said a short prayer. Shortly afterward, both set off on their errand as originally planned.

The Archbishop of Mexico had been taken seriously ill while visiting Lima. The physicians called into attendance on the case had abandoned all hope of recovery. Father Cyprian, a friend of the

the dying man, who was in great pain and very restless. He was suffering from pleurisy.

"Brother Martin, place your hand here on my side. The anguish is unbearable."

Martin's lips were moving in prayer. The eyes of twenty people closely followed him. Then he placed his hand upon the exact spot where the pain was the greatest. Instantly the Archbishop was cured. Everyone in the room intoned the *Te Deum* in thanksgiving for the Archbishop's recovery.

When Father Cyprian sought to thank Brother Martin — he had vanished. Later he found him in the convent and asked him why he had been so ill at ease.

"The room was filled with curious onlookers," explained Martin. "I would have liked to have been left alone with the Archbishop. I prefer not to have people present when there is a cure."

13
Peru's Apostle of Social Service

The complaints within the Convent of the Holy Rosary continued to rumble. In an effort to establish a semblance of order, Father Provincial sent for Brother Martin.

He explained that in the future he was given permission to tend to the sick and poor in town. Unfortunately, however, he would now have to close the convent to all of his patients. Henceforth, they would have to seek refuge elsewhere. The rules of enclosure had to be strictly observed. Nor would Martin hereafter be permitted to use his cell as an infirmary.

Naturally Brother Martin was greatly distressed by this turn of events. How would he be able to come to the aid of the sick and dying? He had looked upon this as an opportunity to be of greater service to his fellow man.

But, being essentially an obedient and docile religious, Martin refrained from saying anything. He kept his thoughts to himself. Now that his superior had spoken, he would carry out the command with utmost fidelity.

Martin went at once to visit his married sister. He asked her consent to bring the most urgent cases to her home. There he knew his beloved sick would be tenderly nursed and cared for. Then he made the rounds of wealthy friends. Again, he found charitable men and women who were willing to open their houses until the day when Brother Martin could establish a permanent center.

The exodus of the sick took place at once. The friars ceased their grumbling. They had their beloved convent to themselves once more. The danger of disease had been eliminated.

Brother Martin tended strictly to his own affairs. He gave no one further cause for dissatisfaction.

Late one night, he hurried home from an urgent sick call. The alley was black. He stumbled over an inanimate object lying at his feet. Martin investigated and found the prostrate form of a dying man, weltering in his own blood. Martin tore off his white scapular in an effort to stem the flow of blood.

The gates of the city were locked. His sister lived too far away for him to transport the man such a distance. There remained but one alternative. He would have to carry the wounded Indian, who had been stabbed in the back, to the convent. Martin realized it was but a matter of hours for the bleeding victim. He doubted whether his newfound patient would live to see the dawn.

In the convent, everyone had been in bed for hours. Martin lifted the moaning Indian onto his own straw pallet. He did not leave his side during the night, counting every pulsebeat and nursing him with the gentle affection of a mother.

Early the next morning, Father Provincial sent for Martin. He was never to know who had reported him. But someone had taken the pains to notify Father Provincial as soon as the greater silence had come to an end. Father Provincial and Father Prior were present. Martin was told that he had broken the rule and been flagrantly disobedient. Father Provincial reprimanded him roundly for housing the Indian — after he had been warned it must not happen again.

Brother Martin was not afforded an opportunity to excuse himself or explain the incident. Instead, he was given a very severe penance which he would have to perform before the brethren in the chapter room.

Brother Martin remained silent. According to rule, he prostrated himself — face forward — in sign of humble submission. Having made his *venia* — he rose, kissed the Provincial's scapular and silently left the room.

Brother Martin had the Indian moved to his sister's house. During the course of the afternoon, Father Provincial passed Brother Martin in the corridor. He was feeling somewhat ashamed of himself for having been so harsh in his admonition of Martin. He stopped him.

"Why, brother. . . I have never seen you look so unhappy. What's the matter? It was my duty to punish you for your lack of obedience. I am sorry for having hurt your feelings and trust I'll never again be called upon to talk to you as I was obliged to do this morning."

Martin knelt in the corridor. In his naive and childlike manner, he said: "I am sorry that I caused so much trouble and disturbed the brethren. You are right, father. I am very much upset. There is an issue which sorely puzzles me. I do not seem to be able to solve it. All day I have been wondering what to think.

"In the novitiate, we were taught that the precept of charity was a commandment given us by Christ, Himself; that charity came before obedience. Last night, I was put to the test: whether I should obey and leave the Indian to die on the road; or be prompted by charity to save his life and do all I could for his miserable soul.

"I really do not know what to do in the future. Was I wrong in setting aside an order given by obedience? Or did I do rightly by following a precept of charity?"

Father Provincial was deeply moved by these simple words. He had always had a keen admiration for Brother Martin. From the first he had understood what an exceptional person this Negro was. Suddenly he was ashamed of the friars; ashamed of their worldly attitude. He knew better than they that, though the convent had experienced a tremendous influx of people, never once had any of them had to do without food or clothing.

Looking at the kneeling figure, he remarked slowly: "Brother. . . you were perfectly right. It is I who was wrong to condemn you. Charity comes before obedience. In the future, you need never again hesitate. Let charity always rule and guide your life. You can never go wrong if that is your beacon.

"From now on, I intend to leave you free to plan your own life and to tend to your sick and dying as you deem best."

Brother Martin's joy was so great that he hardly knew what he was doing. He leaned forward and kissed the feet of his superior, thanking him profusely.

He immediately went into town and made arrangements for securing two adjoining houses plus another outside the city. These could be converted into hospitals for his beloved sick.

While Brother Martin was visiting his patients, the members of Holy Rosary Convent were assembled in chapter. Father Provincial told the community what he thought of their lack of religious spirit. He held Brother Martin up to them as a model and an example. He let them know that Brother Martin's philanthropic endeavors were no longer to be interfered with by petty jealousies. Their criticism and faultfinding would have to come to an end.

Having complete confidence in Brother Martin's judgment, in the future he would be entirely free to do what he felt was best for the honor and glory of God and suffering humanity. Father Provincial took the occasion to impress upon his listeners the fact that this exceptional privilege had been gained by Martin's hidden humility — not by argument, by speech, by excuses or self-defense.

The community was astonished. Many could not understand how a simple lay brother, who had been obliged to wait for nine years as a tertiary before being admitted within the order as a mere lay brother, now commanded such respect. They wondered how it was that Brother Martin had achieved complete independence; why he had been told to act in any manner he saw fit.

Though his understanding superiors were never again to interfere, realizing the greatness of this genius, the brethren remained a bit doubtful.

106

But Martin's years of hidden service were to prove to be stepping-stones to still greater ventures. From then on — his days were to become more crowded; his responsibilities the more demanding.

Brother Martin had tasted misunderstanding and contempt. He knew what it meant to be ridiculed, ostracized and shoved to the last place. He had felt and endured the rebuffs. He had been cruelly hurt. After all, he was human. He had his feelings. Yet Martin had known how to control and master them. He hid his emotions; then turned them toward God.

These years of trial had come to a very sudden end. Father Provincial's public avowal of his keen admiration for Brother Martin and his unexpected position of trust had changed things overnight.

Lima — the City of Kings — was a hotbed of iniquity. There were thousands of wealthy Spaniards. The aristocrats of Lima lived in colonial palaces. Their homes had exquisitely carved balconies; beautifully tiled patios; walls hung with priceless brocades; rooms furnished with works of art.

The Spanish Viceroy and his entourage were surrounded with all the pomp and splendor of Old World courts. Their churches and cathedrals were richly adorned with gold and silver, elaborate wood carvings and paintings by the world's greatest masters.

Money flowed like wine. Fortunes were spent on festivities. Bejewelled party gowns and pearl-embroidered shoes were seen night after night at great banquets, which started at ten o'clock in the evening and lasted until dawn. Eight-and ten-course dinners were the order of the day.

By the year 1553, the University of San Marcos had opened its doors as a seat of learning. It had been modeled after the University of Salamanca. Naturally, it was only for the sons of the well-to-do. The poor had no place in the daily lives of the Spaniards. They were nonexistent. Why should they be concerned with problems which did not interest them?

Peru was a haven of beauty with its sky-pointing Andes, its flower-bedecked fields and its rivers abounding with fish. There were sports of every kind; hunting in the mountains; fishing in the rivers, lakes and the Pacific Ocean. There were excursions to be made to the ruins of famous Inca fortresses and towns.

For those who wished to find a good excuse to stay away from Sunday Mass, there were the cockfights. These started at ten o'clock in the morning and lasted till the evening *Angelus.* Sunday afternoons and on holidays, there were bullfights — with the *toreros* coming all the way from Spain or Mexico. Life in Lima was neither dull nor monotonous.

While the rich lived like royalty — the poor starved. The Indians, Negroes and mulattos had no opportunity for bettering their miserable lives. Beggars brazenly demanded help at church doors. Whining women rang doorbells, pleading for scraps of food for their starving infants. Thieving children roamed the streets, stealing fruits and flowers. Murderers sang their hymns of hate. Night was a cloak for crime. People were unmercifully stabbed in the back.

No one suffered more anguish than did Brother Martin at the appalling picture of crime and evil. He knew who was the cause for all this misery and despair. He saw his own people — the Negroes and the Indians — ground to dust by the haughty, high-living Spaniards. Lima was overrun with orphans, homeless boys and girls and unwanted babies born out of wedlock.

Martin, who had himself experienced the fierce pangs of being an unwanted child, knew what suffering meant. His heart reached out in a practical love for all those who suffered so cruelly; towards all ages, all creeds, all races.

Strange as it seemed, Brother Martin had friends everywhere. No door in Lima was ever closed in his face. He was always welcomed.

First and foremost in his affections came the people of his own race. Time after time, the Negroes had rebelled at their cruel treatment. There had been bloodshed and even death. The Spaniards were deeply resented. They were shunned by young and old, alike. Yet when Martin came down the alley, where the Negroes lived in primitive huts, they were glad to see him.

Sometimes he stayed to help build a new *rucas* settlement — constructed of rushes woven on a framework of wooden poles, with openings left at each end of the roof to permit the smoke to escape.

In their eyes, Brother Martin was bone of their bone and their blood ran in his veins. Even the Incas and other Indian tribes felt friendly toward Martin. He had taken their side. At times, he had even fought for them. In turn, they entrusted him with their utmost confidence.

Martin's remarkable talent as physician and surgeon had broken all racial ties, eradicated all barriers. Poverty, sickness and worry proved excellent levelers. Viceroys, governors and generals came knocking at his door. He found a relief for every ill and a cure for every ailment.

What this simple doctor did for humanity is, in itself, a moving and heartwarming story. His exploits in the field of social service form one of the most glorious chapters of 16th century philanthropy in the western hemisphere. Martin de Porrez was the New World's great pioneer philanthropist. He was to lay the keystone for all future American charitable activities.

The problems confronting Martin were many and varied. His sick were increasing by leaps and bounds. The city hospital and the three other buildings he had set aside for this purpose were all badly overcrowded. He was faced with the problem of finding additional housing.

On just such a day, while walking rapidly and pondering what next he might do, he was accosted by a well-dressed woman wrapped in a brightly colored shawl. She stopped him. Martin was astonished. Spanish ladies never spoke to men in the street.

Before he realized what had happened, she exclaimed: "For the love of God — take my baby, Brother Martin. I have not the heart to do away with him. I know he will be safe with you."

Before Martin could recover from his surprise, the woman had vanished. In his arms he now clutched a tiny infant. What a strange picture the two made — the Negro doctor contrasted by the tiny, white, helpless bundle. He knew there was no use in bringing a crying infant to the convent. Thus he retraced his steps and carried the baby to his sister Juana.

Somehow, the news was quickly broadcast that Brother Martin accepted unwanted babies. He, who could never refuse anyone in need, now found himself the father of orphans. Destitute mothers followed him throughout the streets of the city. They brought to him the half-famished babies they were too poor to feed, or the unwanted infants born out of wedlock. Martin opened wide his arms. His benevolence took on a new aspect.

Soon Juana's home was too small to hold the growing numbers. Then a vacant lot adjoining her property was acquired. People quickly grew accustomed to the sight of Brother Martin, carrying two — or sometimes even three babies — toward the new foundling home.

This was the first time in the history of the New World that anyone had ever been interested in the fate of unwanted babies. Hundreds of thousands of newborn infants had found a watery grave. The Rimac River, pouring into the Pacific, made a convenient burial ground. Slaves had to toil. Negro girls had to work. No one had the time or the means to care for babies born out of wedlock. Besides, Spanish grandees disclaimed the parentage of any dusky progeny. Few of the women had the courage to cling to their offspring.

Brother Martin knew life and its seamy, sordid side. He had no intention of tolerating the fact that rich men could sin but thereafter bear no responsibility for the harsh consequences of their acts. The poor had their hands tied. Without money, nothing could be done. His hungry babies cried for food. His hungry babies had to be housed and fed. Their lusty little lungs made themselves heard by day and by night.

Brother Martin canvassed from house to house. He rarely asked for the lady of the home. It was to the head of the household that he spoke. Brother Martin must have been very vehement and very direct in his approach. Apparently he minced no words. For, few Spaniards in Lima could afford to listen to his burning accusations.

If they had any hearts — and most of them could be and were moved by his pleas — they felt a sense of horror and shame at the picture he painted. He let them know it was now up to them to atone for the appalling evil that had been done. The very least they could do now would be to help build suitable homes for these helpless and wronged infants by way of reparation.

With available funds, Brother Martin bought land close to the Dominican Convent of the Magdalena. He carefully made a blueprint. His plans were well-laid. Every detail was minutely explored. However, no architect could be found who would build exactly to Martin's specifications. Thus it was that Brother Martin, himself, also served as architect for the first true foundling asylum in the New World.

Many people protested what they deemed an utter waste of time and money. Why should such an expensive building be erected for dying infants? By the merest chance of fortune, these unwanted babies had managed to escape death by drowning. Who could possibly care whether they lived or died?

Next — the structure, itself, came in for a severe round of criticism. Why should foundlings be endowed with a luxurious abode? Who ever heard of such huge windows and vast, open verandas? Was he building a palace?

People shook their heads. Brother Martin had been given too much power. The money had gone to his head. They predicted he would soon see what a white elephant he had on his hands. The babies would die. Even amongst the wealthy, infant mortality was appalling. So, how could he possibly expect to save the destitute?

Brother Martin was unperturbed. "These babies are my responsibility. I have my own system of infant hygiene. You have yours. I believe in sunshine and fresh air."

Into the spacious and airy dormitories, attractive cribs were placed. When the sun shone, the windows were thrown open. The children spent most of their day, basking along vine-entwined verandas.

To encourage mothers to deposit their unwanted babies, the baby door was invented. From the inside — nothing could be seen. A revolving turnstile was fitted with a little basket large enough to hold a year-old baby. Whenever the bell was rung, the basket would be swung toward the street. Into this receptacle, the unwanted infant was placed; while on the other side of the turnstile, the foundling would be warmly received and given immediate medical attention.

Every once in a while, a poor bewildered mother — on hearing of the wonderful care given to all babies by Brother Martin — would leave an older child. Even so, no one was ever to be refused admission or be turned away.

Contrary to the predictions of the town gossips, the white elephant on which so much money and effort had been squandered proved to be an enormous success. The venture grew. The half-famished babies were well cared for. Instead of dying — they lived happily at the orphanage to become healthy youngsters.

Brother Martin had not been an idle dreamer. He was a realist who looked toward the future. These children would someday become the hope of his nation. They were the destined leaders of every class and every race. These were not just foundlings or mere castaways. To him each infant was a distinct personality, an important member of society. As such he would care for it, tending to its medical, moral and spiritual needs.

Brother Martin's venture worked. Everyone marveled. Rich and poor, alike, came to visit the foundling home. There was no racial segregation. It was first come, first served. The Negroes, Indians and Spanish babies lay in identical cribs. They were fed the same food, cared for in an identical manner.

No preference was shown to anyone in this model nursery. In Brother Martin's eyes — all were equal. They were all his children.

14
Many Sided Martin

Martin's responsibilities grew. As he looked about him, he became apprehensive; apprehensive because the sickly, dying infants thrust into his arms all lived. They far outnumbered anything anticipated. He had been prepared to receive a few. Instead, the hundreds were multiplied into thousands. To this list was now added a new category. Often entire families were left orphaned by plague or malaria.

Once the foundling home had been established, it soon became known that Brother Martin never turned away any child. Daily a procession of tots of varying ages awaited at the door. Martin lacked the courage to turn these helpless waifs away. Where would they go? To whom could they turn? His heart was so loving, his charity so great that he somehow managed to find the ways and means for accepting them. This, of necessity, meant the crowding of his beloved foundlings.

His babies were now outgrowing their cribs. They were crawling and running about, requiring constant care. The more they grew — the greater the difficulties that arose. Martin was a firm believer in segregating children. He felt that babies should be kept to themselves with the older children provided for elsewhere.

His next step was to make special provision for the nursery-age group. For these he built another home, where they could romp and play in a model kindergarten. Here not only was there sufficient space; but they also had all the fresh air and sunshine they needed. There were toys to keep the little hands occupied and out of mischief. The gardens were shaded, the lawns as beautiful as if the home had been designed for the children of the rich.

Special attention was accorded those of preschool age. Martin felt that these children had reached him at the most crucial period of their lives. Habits acquired and methods assimilated during these formative years would have lasting effects throughout a lifetime. They were shown how to dress, how to care for themselves, how to act. In addition, they were taught their ABC's.

Martin's critics were virulent. They could see no good, whatsoever, coming from such a program. But Martin no longer hesitated. He no longer would listen to what anyone had to say. Instead, he was driven by an inner urge to serve humanity, to aid youth. To do so constructively, he realized he must start at the beginning and work his way up. But, once having done so, he was astonished by the amazing results he had been able to achieve.

There still remained one group outside of Martin's sphere of influence. He was greatly concerned because the local prisons were crowded with thieving children. Forced to do so by hunger — they broke into homes, climbed fruit trees and scaled walls. When caught, they were housed in the same jail as habitual criminals. No one had provided for the youthful gang-age group. These roaming bands of wild, immoral children were the terror of the populace.

Martin realized that these hardened youngsters — daily exposed to every danger — were the ones most likely to be waylaid and led astray. He felt that these particular children would be much better fitted to face life if they received some sort of education. He wanted to see them equipped to handle life's problems.

These were the youths to whom Martin would give a high school and college education. They would have a place of their own. Thus, during the vital years of adolescence, they would be sheltered. By daily contact with kindly and helpful teachers and wise spiritual advisors, their sordid lives could be readjusted.

He would plan a curriculum which would divide their day into study and practical knowledge. There would be workshops, where boys could learn carpentry, tailoring, farming, chemistry and medicine. By preparing its wayward youth for a suitable career, Lima would also be ridding itself of a dangerous criminal element.

No sooner had Martin announced his intention of building a college to be devoted to gang-age youths than civic and ecclesiastical authorities rose in horror. He had overstepped the boundaries of propriety. This was absolutely preposterous. Who had ever heard of educating the down-and-outs? What utter nonsense, indeed — teaching the children of slaves and paupers to be scholars! Paupers had no need for education.

Martin fought his battle for higher education single-handed. Such an idea had never before entered the heads of either the Spanish officials or local ecclesiastics — though, in the history of the church, the idea was not new. Irish missionaries had done the same throughout Gaul and Helvetia. This was how they had evangelized the savage barbarians.

Brother Martin earnestly assured his opponents that every last *centavo* put into the venture would be worth its weight in gold. His own two years of schooling as a lad of eight had enabled him to make the grade. Those two brief years had fitted him for his career as a doctor. By knowing how to read and write, his entire life had been changed. Why should not the same advantages be given these deprived children?

After mature deliberation and many hours of prayer, Brother Martin went to see the Archbishop of Lima. He sought to secure his approbation. The Archbishop had already heard about the unusual enterprise. He knew of the unfavorable comments and the criticism. But he listened carefully to what Martin had to say. He studied in minute detail the long prospectus, giving a full account of the proposed plan of studies.

Finally, when it came time for Martin to leave, His Excellency wholeheartedly gave his approval to so noble an enterprise — though he stipulated that Martin would have to shoulder the full responsibility for its outcome. If the venture proved a failure, he alone would be held to blame.

Brother Martin was also advised that he would personally have to arrange for the school's financing. This was nothing new to Brother Martin. In the past, it had always been his lot to assume all financial responsibility. He was quite willing to do so again. Only — this time — Brother Martin was determined that the college should become a project which would receive the support

115

and backing of all the prominent citizens of the city of Lima.

He approached the Viceroy and the Governor. They were requested to become patrons. The list of civil dignitaries who became sponsors was long and imposing. No one had the heart to say "no" to Martin. Everyone wished to participate. Though the contributions were large and many donations had been exceedingly generous, the sum still was not sufficient for the undertaking of so vast an enterprise. Finally, Martin sought the aid of an old-time friend.

Often in the past, when destitute or in need of medicine or herbs, Brother Martin had visited Don Mateo Pastor. He was a wealthy merchant and owner of the largest drugstore in Lima. Here was a man who had never been known to say "no" to any of Martin's petitions. Though Martin usually waited until the last moment before seeking his help, on this special visit he told Don Mateo at once that he had not come for medicines — but for money, instead. For a very large sum this time. He was still 200,000 *Pesos* short of his goal.

Don Mateo bade Martin wait to tell his story. He wished his wife to hear what he had to say. The elderly couple — Don Mateo and his wife, Doña Francisca — were childless. They had always hoped to have a large family of their own.

As Brother Martin unfolded his story, revealing his dreams and ambitions, they listened enthralled. They felt he was right in his plan for a beautiful dwelling, which would constitute the only home these boys would ever know. They wanted to have a share in the project. They wished to help provide these underprivileged children with a real home.

Without the slightest hesitation, Don Mateo Pastor and his wife gave Martin the vitally needed 200,000 *Pesos*. They told him to spend it as he felt best; to do with it whatever he most wanted.

When Holy Cross College was completed, it was a monument to those who had held unwavering faith in Martin's farseeing vision. Though kindly Don Mateo Pastor and his wife were to remain its greatest benefactors, everyone in Lima felt he had made his own personal contribution. Rich and poor, alike, had all given something.

The college was run very differently from anything hitherto known in those days. Brother Martin looked into the future. The foundations he laid then were to last throughout the centuries. The plans he formulated in the 16th century were still to hold good in the 20th century.

Martin introduced many far-reaching innovations in education. He carefully selected an efficient staff. The men and women employed were given a salary, which was entirely unheard of at the time. Those employed had a right to earn a living wage. Being neither nuns nor priests, they were entitled to be paid adequate remuneration for their work.

Secondly, Martin did not wish to have incompetent men and women handling the welfare of his children. A paid staff could easily be discharged and replaced by better teachers. He could not risk having his educational venture ruined by misfits. He would personally select his co-workers and pay them fair wages for their services.

Soon he had an efficient staff of professors, a resident doctor and nurse and a priest who acted as chaplain. The only entrance requirement for admission was poverty. Neither race nor creed mattered in the slightest. The very best to be had was placed at the ready disposal of these pupils. They soon learned useful professions and were carefully moulded into self-respecting citizens.

Brother Martin was a born leader. He was made for responsibility. His was the intuitive art which knew how to seek out able assistants. Martin never could have carried on the superhuman work he had embraced had he not known how to entrust his authority to others.

The building of Holy Cross College was a typical example of his methods for achieving success. He took upon himself the heaviest burdens. It was he who personally planned and laid out Holy Cross College. It was he, who during the construction days, supervised the hundreds of workers who carried out his orders. He saw to it that every phase of the building was just what he had planned.

Once the building had been completed, his staff organized and the program of studies agreed on — then Brother Martin invited Don Mateo Pastor to assist him. Side by side, they watched the progress of those first weeks. Martin initiated the elderly merchant into the ways of handling youth, of supervising the faculty and of contacting the outside world. Then Martin planned to retire to assume other burdens just as pressing.

Don Mateo Pastor and his kindly wife were just the sort of people needed to gain the confidence of the young students. Both boys and girls were admitted, though they were segregated. The boys spent much time learning professions which would aid them in later life. The girls were taught the skills of homemaking: cooking, sewing and housekeeping.

Brother Martin was a firm believer in wholesome recreation. He saw to it that there were fiestas. He wanted his boys and his girls to meet. They were bound to be compatible; for they had so much in common. He saw in his young people suitable material for the founding of future Christian homes. Many of these pupils, in fact, later married the same girls who had attended their former history or writing classes. When either one of the young couple was too poor to contemplate marriage, it was Brother Martin who would provide a dowry.

In those days, it was customary for parents to provide an adequate sum of money which would be given to the future bridegroom. This helped toward outfitting the home. With this nest egg, the bride secured her personal clothing and the household linens required to start a new ménage. Convents had no other form of endowment. The dowry of a postulant was carefully invested. It helped to feed her and tide her over during periods of illness.

Brother Martin took unto himself many of the burdens of parenthood. He felt that the children of Holy Cross College had every right to marry if they wished to do so; while others of their number would desire to become nuns or priests.

Brother Martin would never permit poverty to stand in the way of his young people's future happiness. In order to overcome this monetary obstacle, he established a special fund. Thus the neediest boys or girls, who would have experienced great difficulty in earning their household money, could draw 4,000 *Pesos*. It was all done in such a modest manner that no one was conscious of the fact that he had been thus aided. Yet through Brother Martin's efforts, arrangements were made whereby fifty-four of his children each, in turn, received a dowry of 4,000 *Pesos*.

Never had there been such a champion of the afflicted. Martin had checked crime amongst Peruvian youth. He had provided for the wants of Indians, Negroes and Spaniards. He had known that the day would come when he would be faced with the grave problem of what to do with young mothers — the girls who had fallen by the wayside; the girls who wished to mend their ways and do something constructive with their lives.

For these he finally found a home — a place where they could go and be rehabilitated. A place where no one would mock them or point a finger of shame in their face. Here they were asked no questions; only mothered and cared for. No time limit was set for their stay. They were welcome to remain permanently if they so elected. Otherwise work would be found for them in some Spanish home or store.

Once the girls had been provided for, Martin next felt obliged to do something on behalf of the aged — those men and women broken with the weight of the years and enfeebled by disease. There were so many elderly that it required several institutions to house and care for them. But, again, with all the strategy of a general preparing for battle — Brother Martin knew when to strike, when to appeal, whom to approach for help.

What heartwarming moments they were for Brother Martin when those tottering with age seized his hand to thank him for the security they had never expected to know. Never again would they feel the pangs of hunger, or endure the humiliation of being forced to beg.

The territory covered by Martin's charities was so vast that it was humanly impossible for him to keep a personal eye on everything. Finally, in desperation, he turned to two dear friends. He named them his companions and assistants. One was a Dominican lay brother and son of a Spanish nobleman called Juan

Masias; the other a young man of Lima named Juan Vasquez. Between them, they divided the city — making methodical rounds, supervising, reporting and controlling.

But Martin insisted on retaining for himself that section of the city set aside for the slaves. Those too ill to be transported to the hospitals he nursed in their poor adobe hovels. Later, he had a special hospital built for the exclusive care of these slaves. He, himself, had tasted the bitterness of being repudiated. He knew that no matter how hard and long he insisted, his nurses and doctors would not treat the slaves as equals or accord them the same care they gave to other patients. In a hospital of their own, they would no longer be neglected.

Martin knew how to ferret out the poverty-stricken Negroes. He personally knew by name both old and young, men and women. They were all especially dear to him. He loved them as if they were members of his own family. Their appalling misery made him also suffer.

He could not bear to see squalor or dirt. With his broom, he swept away the rubbish which littered their doorways. He had masons come to mend the cracked adobe walls, which admitted the scorching sun and torrential rains. He was always quick to notice the threadbare shawls or tattered skirts and made a point of having them replaced.

Usually when he left that squalid section of the city, he would be minus either his cloak or scapular. For he had seen some half-naked protege who needed these more than he did.

The Negroes were Brother Martin's chosen people. His love for them was one of predilection. When they were lonely or homesick, he would sit with them and cheer them. During their illnesses, he kept watch by their poor pallets. When everyone else abandoned them, fearful of catching the dreaded plague, it was Martin who cooled their burning brows. When death came, he sought a priest to pray over them and bring them the Last Sacraments. When their sad lives came to an end, he himself dug their graves and wiped the tears of the mourners.

Sometimes he would wander about the streets, looking for the address of a former Spanish grandee. Somehow, he would learn that poverty and want had come knocking at that door. Too proud to beg, too haughty to ask for help — these aristocratic women gradually succumbed to the charity of Brother Martin. His tact was such that others felt they were doing him a favor by accepting his gifts.

With all these many and varied activities, it was small wonder that Brother Martin soon required the services of a treasurer to handle the donations that poured into his cell. Weekly he distributed 4,000 *Pesos* to the needy. Each month, 16,000 *Pesos* were handed out to the poor. No one ever really knew just how and where all that money came from. Though large sums frequently passed through Martin's hands, he was far from reckless. Nor did he ever squander foolishly any sums confided to his charities.

During the course of a few years, which encompassed the worst period of the economic depression, Brother Martin supported over 650 families in Lima, alone: 650 homes about to be wrecked by poverty and want; by illness and lack of work.

Brother Martin felt that there was no greater joy on earth than that of a happy home. He, who had never been fortunate enough to know such personal happiness, was now the most ardent advocate of the stabilizing influence of the home. He was a firm believer that no one could supplant the care or affection of a loving mother.

On all occasions, Martin strove to preserve the sanctity of the home; to prevent the separation of children from their parents. He looked upon foundling homes and kindergartens as deplorable necessities, at best. Whenever he could, he would place his babies with women who wanted children. Martin felt that the Christian home was the one great bulwark against the evils of the times. Thus, in Martin's day, the home was safeguarded. No one ever dared to oust a tenant without facing his personal wrath.

Martin maintained close communication with local Spanish officials. However, this was not due either to love or respect for these corrupt political appointees; but because it enabled him to keep a closer eye on their evil ways. He felt these were the very men who had destroyed Peru. Their greed for gold had made them cruel. They were the ones who had exploited helpless Indians and littered the country with hundreds of thousands of starving natives.

Martin was all too well aware of these conditions. He had seen how taxes had been raised on even the poorest adobe hovels; how men and women were battling for life without food — facing starvation and disease. The prisons of Peru were overflowing with men and women arrested for stealing for sustenance. Their crime: looting the gardens of the rich. The depression had reached its height. Yet the government still did nothing to alleviate the evil.

Martin decided that these socially-wronged men and women were the ones no one would ever be able to reach unless something were done for them as a group. He planned to aid the starving who were too poor to pay for food. They would no longer be forced to scale walls and steal fruit. He would start a back-to-the-land movement. . . an agrarian crusade.

The unemployed would be given something constructive to do on their own behalf. In exchange for hard work and wholehearted participation in a shared community effort, they would be promised a plentiful supply of food in the future.

On the outskirts of Lima, there was an arid wasteland called Limatambo. For practically nothing, Brother Martin succeeded in buying this land to give to his poor.

Throughout the city, notices were posted — inviting the cooperation of all who wished to take part in the endeavor. The land at Limatambo was to be plowed under and olive trees and fig trees planted for the exclusive use of the poor. Those who participated in the planting would be the ones who would share in the profits of the harvest.

Such a public declaration on Martin's part required heroic courage. It meant facing a hostile world of Spaniards, who had previously decreed that work in either field or garden was to be strictly reserved for slaves and not permitted by free human beings.

Accompanied by a group of faithful volunteers — bared to the waist — Brother Martin began to dig one dawn on the arid outskirts of Lima. Soon Martin was joined by thousands of others who eagerly followed the example he set. The cruel, hot sun beat on their bent backs. But Martin had prepared lotions of salt and vinegar. He insisted that the men now rub their bodies with this solution in order to protect themselves from the swarms of mosquitoes.

Martin promised these workers that never again would they have to fear the pangs of hunger. Henceforth, this land of promise would belong to the poor of Lima and food in abundance would be theirs.

Four hundred years later, gnarled and twisted olive trees — with branches bowed to the ground by the silvery weight of years — proved to the world that Martin had kept his promise. Brother Martin's fig trees and olive groves still bore rich fruit; while empty prisons attested mutely to the fact that the agrarian movement had also been one of successful rehabilitation.

15
The Consummation

Brother Martin's activities furnished unforgettable pen pictures of a very remarkable career. Nothing had been overlooked by him, nothing forgotten. There now remained only one category that had been heretofore neglected: the Indians who lived in the High Andes.

These were the farmers who tilled the terraced gardens laid out centuries before by their Inca ancestors. They eked out a miserable existence, laboring hard — hauling the guano from nearby islands up the steep mountain passes in order to fertilize their barren little plots of land.

There were also the herders of the alpacas. These animals, with their long coats of wool, subsisted off the tough grass of the highlands. From them the herders obtained much of the wool that was used for clothing. In still another mountainous area, there were the miners of the gold, silver and copper.

The once proud and happy Incas had been reduced to a subjugated slave race. Brother Martin knew that the sick and aged, when bedridden, possessed neither bedding nor medicines. They had been woefully neglected.

This time, Brother Martin personally made the rounds of the Spanish nobility. The wife of the Viceroy was his friend. He reminded her that it was scarcely fitting for her husband and children to ride in a gold-and-scarlet chariot with footmen attired in elaborate livery — followed by knights mounted on horses bedecked with harnesses, flashing with silver, and velvet trappings studded with jewels — while their people were starving.

He hoped the Vicereine would interest herself in a worthwhile venture. He would like the ladies of Lima to prepare medical kits; to collect used sheets and blankets. He, in turn, would provide the necessary medical supplies; they the rest.

Thus Brother Martin became the first medical missionary of the New World. He hired llama caravans, which were packed with medicines, bedding and all the necessities for relieving the afflicted in the poverty-stricken mountain hamlets.

Another great concern of Brother Martin was for the welfare of the missionary priests, who had been sent over by the Spanish Crown by the hundreds. These dedicated men had no other desire than to evangelize and preach the gospels of Christ.

Though they had been promised full aid and support — once they reached the New World, they were quickly forgotten. Their appeals for assistance went unheeded; their letters unanswered. Their parishioners consisted of destitute Indians whom the *conquistadores* had plundered and robbed. These missionaries were now starving and did not even have the use of vestments or altar linens.

Again, Brother Martin turned to his friends. For, by now, everyone loved him and knew that if he appealed to them, it was bound to be for an urgent and worthwhile cause.

He founded an Altar Society — an organization that took charge of just such cases and met many needs within the parish. Instead of brocaded evening dresses, Brother Martin pleaded for vestments.

Instead of fine linens and laces for sheets and pillows, he requested altar linens. Once more, the women of Lima took to their needles to sew industriously and work hard in support of a worthy cause. Thursdays and Fridays were devoted to the Altar Society.

Brother Martin found that his charities had expanded to such a degree that it was now necessary to organize them. Henceforth, donations received on Tuesdays and Wednesdays would be given to aid the local poor. Men, women and children would benefit therefrom. On Sundays, the alms received were to be used to buy sheets, blankets, medicine and clothing for the bedridden mountain folk.

Toward the end of his life, Martin felt he was morally responsible for all those who had passed through his hands over the years. For the destitute, who had been so poor they had not even had relatives. For his motherless and fatherless orphans, who counted entirely on him. Whenever any of these died, he felt a personal responsibility to pray for them. During their lifetime, he also felt they needed prayers.

Thus, in the future, the alms collected on Mondays and Saturdays would be sent to poor priests in parishes and convents. These padres, in return, would be asked to say special Masses for the dead as well as for the living.

While Brother Martin's footsteps had been hounded by the poor and suffering, he also had a dedicated following of the most outstanding and influential people of Peru.

Amongst his best friends, he counted both the Governor and the Viceroy. The wife of the Viceroy had taken active participation in many of Martin's philanthropies. Her husband, Don Luis Fernandez de Bobadilla, kept Brother Martin supplied with ample pocket money for his good works. He felt that this lowly Negro would succeed in contacting needy men and women about whom he might never otherwise hear. He had implicit confidence and trust in Martin's judgment.

The Governor of Peru, Don Juan de Figueroa, loved Martin like a brother. He, too, was generous with his money.

On one occasion, when suddenly taken very ill in the middle of the night, he sent messengers to fetch Brother Martin. As the humble lay brother left the convent, he found the state chariot awaiting in readiness to rush him to the Governor's bedside. The Governor was dying. He had asked for Martin. Martin assured the liveried footmen that there really was no need to hurry, no urgency whatever. But orders were orders. Brother Martin found himself whisked away, nevertheless.

When he reached the governor's palace, the perturbed nobleman was pleased to see his friend. His Excellency then asked to be left alone with Martin in order to make arrangements for his funeral. He told Brother Martin where he would like to be buried, seeking his advice and begging him to break the news to his family.

Brother Martin just smiled. He assured Don Juan that there was no need at all for preparing so hastily for death; for his ailment was a mere passing malady. Brother Martin went on to predict that His Excellency would live for many years more. In fact, that he would outlive Brother Martin, himself.

Brother Martin's prediction came to pass. It was not until sixteen years following Martin's death that the Governor of Peru, himself, passed away.

The Governor had so mourned the loss of his close friend, Brother Martin, that when his last hour on earth came — he had but one wish. He requested to be laid to rest side by side with the humble Negro lay brother. He could think of no greater joy, no greater honor than this. Father Provincial granted the Governor his last wish.

When Brother Martin had died, he was laid to rest beneath the floor of his simple cell. But, thanks to the munificence of the Governor, that cell would now become a beautiful chapel. It was here that these two longtime friends were finally to be joined in eternal rest.

Before Brother Martin's span of life came to an end, there were still certain important things he hoped to be able to accomplish in the remaining time allotted him.

In 1634, the city of Lima was disastrously inundated. The Rimac River had overflowed its banks, flooding the town and sweeping away thousands of homes.

Desperate citizens rushed to Brother Martin's side for refuge and help. They implored him to intercede with God. They pleaded that something be done at once to avert the impending catastrophe before it could take place. For a while, it looked as if all Lima might soon be under water; as if the raging river would surely wash what little was left of the town into the Pacific.

Brother Martin had been away, supervising one of his new hospitals erected in an outlying mountain district. Immediately upon his return, he joined the heroic rescue efforts in progress in a valiant attempt to save as many people as humanly possible.

The task of saving lives, however, proved exceedingly dangerous. The current of the river was deadly and swift. Time after time, Martin stood up to his waist in the powerfully surging water. Some of his friends were fearful he might drown, as — time and again — he lost his footing in the turbulent eddies.

The lay brother finally shook his head. "There is nothing any of us can do," he admitted sadly. "The disaster is too great."

Everywhere were heard groans and piercing shrieks of terror. Houses crumpled as if made of cardboard. Above the roar and rumble of the Rimac River came the anguished cries of foundering thousands: "Give us back our city. Save Lima for us."

As Brother Martin reached a dry piazza, he was confronted by the Governor. "Is there nothing you can do?" His Excellency demanded.

Brother Martin searched the agonized faces of his friends. For the first time in his long experience, he — who had dedicated himself to alleviating the suffering of others — was pained by the realization that he was helpless to do anything to solve this present crisis.

Many of Martin's former benefactors surrounded him, turning their grief-stricken faces to his in mute supplication. These were the selfsame people who had gladly opened their hearts and purses to any and all appeals he had made in the past. Now, for once in their lives, they had come to him for help in return. Yet here he stood before them — powerless to act on their behalf to save the day.

Above the roar of the angry flood came the hoarse shouts: "Brother Martin. . . pray. Brother Martin. . . ask God for help. Please be our intercessor."

Brother Martin folded his hands and knelt on the pavement. He closed his eyes and lifted his heart and mind to God.

What he said in prayer no one would ever know. But, during that interval — which seemed like an eternity to the waiting throng — Brother Martin was completely oblivious to the fact that the floodwaters had already reached the land on which he was kneeling. It would only be a matter of minutes before the Church of Las Cabez would be undermined. Its thick walls would crumble and fall as so many others already had done.

Upon opening his eyes, Brother Martin saw three stones. He took one, blessing it in the name of the Holy Trinity; then placed it outside the front door of the church.

Next, he plunged into the swirling waters — holding a stone in each hand. He placed the second stone in several feet of water. The third he threw far away —toward the crest of the flood — where a violent whirlpool engulfed everything in its path.

Instantly the torrent of water ceased rising. By the time Martin had waded back to the Church of Las Cabez, the flood had become stationary.

The frenzied cries of terror changed to shouts of deliverance and joy. Then the grateful mob seized Brother Martin and carried him triumphantly into the Church of Las Cabez, where a *Te Deum* of thanksgiving was intoned.

Soon afterward, the citizens of Lima came to Martin with a petition. To prove their gratitude for the wonderful miracle he had performed, they planned to move the Church of Las Cabez to the safety of the mountainside. Thus, the next time the Rimac overflowed, the church would be in no danger of destruction by flood.

Brother Martin angrily reprimanded his friends, telling them their faith was short-lived. Already they had forgotten what God had done for them. If God had spared their beloved church once, surely He would do so a second time. Brother Martin then foretold that no such catastrophe would ever again devastate Lima; nor the Rimac River once more overflow its banks.

Archbishop Feliciano de la Vega, whom Martin had cured of pleurisy, had returned to Mexico. He felt that he owed the prolongation of his life to Brother Martin's efforts. To show his deep appreciation, he now wished to devote the remaining years of his life to good works and acts of charity.

He had seen what Brother Martin had been able to accomplish in Lima. He had known the town before Martin started his work. He had witnessed the startling change after the miracle worker had made the townsfolk conscious of their obligation toward the sick and poor.

Back in Mexico, the Archbishop had attempted to bring about the same far-reaching reforms Brother Martin had introduced in Lima. But the Archibishop failed. He had no one possessing Martin's zeal or incentive and there were but few who could match his powers of endurance.

The Archbishop had written to Brother Martin, asking him to come to Mexico. Brother Martin had no time left in his crowded days for correspondence. Thus he completely forgot the incident.

The next time the Archbishop of Mexico came to Lima, he sent for Martin at once. He pleaded that he urgently required his services in Mexico. Brother Martin merely laughed, reminding him he was only a simple Negro lay brother with no authority, whatever.

The Archbishop assured Martin that everything he had accomplished to date in Lima was by now so well-organized, his hospitals, his foundling homes, his schools and college could certainly carry on without him for a while. But Brother Martin flatly refused to consider the offer.

However, Archbishop de la Vega was a man who held much influence in high places. He had already approached the Archbishop of Lima, who agreed that it would be an excellent idea to institute the same philanthropic endeavors in Mexico. While the latter had no direct authority over Brother Martin, who was a Dominican, that permission could nevertheless be obtained over

Brother Martin's head. The Archbishop of Lima suggested that Archbishop de la Vega secure leave from the Dominican Provincial.

The Archbishop of Mexico had been one of the greatest benefactors of the Dominican Order. Time after time, when they were in dire want, he had come to their rescue. Now that the Archbishop came with so urgent a request, Father Provincial found his hands tied. Sadly he was forced to give his consent to Martin's transfer. Somehow, he felt that there never had been anyone like Brother Martin. Nor would anyone else ever be able to replace him.

Both the Archbishop and the Provincial decided it might be wisest to keep the matter a secret for the present. If the townsfolk got wind of the affair, there was bound to be an uprising in angry reaction to these unwanted tidings. There was no use in inviting trouble ahead of time. As far as Brother Martin was concerned, both church dignitaries knew the lay brother would unhesitatingly obey the command of his superior.

The Archbishop was delighted by his successful maneuver. He proceeded to make the final arrangements for departure, ordering vast stores of medicines, blankets and shawls to be shipped to his boat.

Only three days prior to the scheduled sailing was Brother Martin advised that he was to leave Lima in the company of the Archbishop of Mexico. Contrary to the Provincial's expectation, Brother Martin appeared not to be in the least surprised by this news. In fact, he acted as if he had known all the details of the preparations well in advance.

The next day, Brother Martin appeared in the convent clad in a brand-new habit. The friars teased their old friend. Most of them had never known Martin to wear anything but a shabby patched and mended habit. By then the news had leaked out that he was soon to sail for Mexico. They asked him if it was in anticipation of the forthcoming voyage that he had discarded his familiar ragged habit for the new one. Martin just laughed.

Then, to a priest whom he loved dearly, Brother Martin remarked: "My dear father, you are very much mistaken. I am not going to wear this habit to Mexico. I contemplate taking another and much longer journey. Since I expect to be buried in this habit, I have decided to try it out to see what it feels like."

Though Martin's words seemed to have been spoken in jest, the priest who heard them was awestruck by the underlying seriousness with which Brother Martin had uttered his astonishing statement.

That very evening, Brother Martin was stricken by a dangerous fever. He was totally incapacitated and forced to go to bed. Though the infirmarian brought him various remedies to alleviate the pain, Brother Martin protested that nothing could help this time. The infirmarian was annoyed. He knew it was just another one of those yearly malaria attacks to which Brother Martin periodically succumbed.

"Please don't waste any medicine on me," pleaded Brother Martin. "There are others who need it more than I do. I shall die of this illness. All remedies are useless. My earthly pilgrimage has ended. My hour to depart has come."

The brother who was nursing Martin shook his head, deciding his patient must be delirious. Then suddenly there was a decided change for the worse. Martin grew very weak.

Hoping to help him regain his appetite and strength, Father Provincial ordered a fowl to be killed immediately and chicken broth administered to the patient.

Apparently Brother Martin overheard the conversation, for he whispered humbly:

"Please do not take the life of one of God's creatures for my sake. I assure you that no matter what you give me, it will not prove of the slightest use. The time has come for me to die. And I am ready to go."

The Archbishop of Mexico had been notified of Martin's passing indisposition. But when he learned there had been a turn for the worse, he immediately cancelled his return passage to Mexico. He went at once to Martin's bedside.

The news spread rapidly throughout Lima. The whole town was plunged into instant mourning. Churches were packed — both by day and throughout the long night — with praying throngs. No one could believe that Brother Martin would die and leave them. He had been the center of their lives for so long, he had become indispensable.

In Brother Martin's humble little cell, friends took turns watching and praying.

A very young priest, who had been one of Martin's most ardent admirers, knelt at the foot of his straw pallet. Aloud he sobbed:

"What am I to do without you to guide me? From the time of my childhood — you have always led me. Now on whom can I lean? To whom shall I turn to show me the way?"

Brother·Martin smiled gently. "Do not grieve, my son. It's God's Holy Will that I die. Who knows? Perhaps, in the end, I shall be of much more use to you in Heaven. I expect to go there. I may be able to do more for you there than here on earth."

Martin's dearest friend, Governor Juan de Figueroa, did not once leave his vigil by the lay brother's side. He had dropped the affairs of state to offer himself in Brother Martin's service.

The Viceroy, Luis Fernandez de Bobadilla, came several times a day to see if there were anything he might be able to do. But Brother Martin was scarcely conscious of what was going on around him. Though he suffered much, he was wrapped in prayer.

On one occasion — for over half an hour — Martin's tiny cell was luminated with a celestial light. Those who attended him saw Brother Martin's poor, tired features transported with joy. He was talking to the Blessed Virgin. She had appeared to him in a vision.

From that moment on — Martin was oblivious to the things of this earth.

Toward evening on the third of November, 1639 — the community bell rang. All those who could tried to find a corner in Martin's cell, while others knelt outside in the corridors. The Archbishop of Mexico recited the prayers for the dying.

Suddenly — Brother Martin sat up. Though in great pain, he looked about him at the faces of those whom he had served so faithfully, so long. In a weakened voice, he humbly asked them to pardon him for the bad example he had given during his life in the convent. Then, exhausted from the effort, he fell back onto the hard straw pallet.

While the community joined the Archbishop in the recitation of the prayers, Brother Martin tightly clutched his crucifix in his emaciated hands. His eyes were bathed in tears as they were fixed on that cross in loving veneration. From time to time, his trembling hands raised the cross to his lips. As he kissed the wounded side of Christ, he seemed to derive renewed strength for his final struggle.

As the Archbishop concluded the prayers for the dying, Martin whispered that he would like to have the Apostles' Creed said. All the community joined in the prayer.

As the words *"Et Homo Factus Est"* were recited in unison, Brother Martin slipped to his eternal reward.

Thence, from out the deep silence of the night, came the heavy clattering and clanging of the bells of Holy Rosary Convent. The bells tolled their sad tale to the hushed multitude.

All the churches of Lima picked up the plaintive refrain. Convents, hospitals, foundling homes and asylums of every type and description rang their bells in this, their shared grief.

Hundreds of thousands of men, women and children fell to their knees. All of Lima. . . all of Peru mourned the passing of a father, friend and benefactor.

At that moment in history — the rich and poor, the great and lowly, the young and old, alike, lost one of the most remarkable men of all times.

By his saintly and selfless life, Brother Martin had taught humanity the much-needed lesson. He believed that the Charity of Christ is all-embracing.

He lived that life — giving to the best of his ability — irrespective of race, color or creed.

PUBLISHERS' NOTE

In an effort to be many-sided in our work, we have tried to present different aspects of religious life and choose the lives of saints outstanding for their time and for their work.

Saint Francis Xavier, the 16th Century Nobleman, gives an excellent picture of his period and times.

While St. Francis of Assisi, the Italian cloth merchant's son was a troubadour at heart and somewhat of a playboy, he in his own inimitable manner led hundreds of thousands to Christ.

We of the Western Hemisphere have a saint all of our own. No one has ever been able to imitate or copy his way of life. That great humanitarian, Saint Martin de Porres, son of a Panamanian Negress and a Spanish nobleman, abandoned by Father and Mother, had the courage to become a physician and become the New World's first builder of hospitals, orphanages and homes for the aged. His love for the poor and down-trodden is one of the most glorious chapters of Latin American philanthropy.

Our book "THE DEAD SPEAK" is of historical value — the story of two heroic, fearless Yugoslav and Hungarian refugees who were aided by the Pope's Children War Relief to reach Brazil to begin life anew.

TRAGEDY IN PARIS is a nun's story. Back in 1930 it was a sensation. Unfortunately today it is an everyday affair, happening to many.

With the Grace of God we plan to bring out more lives of saints — outstanding men and women and at the same time provide material on religious life.

Benziger Sisters Publishing Company
466 East Mariposa Street
Altadena, California 91001

134